Getting It Done

Getting It Done

LEADING ACADEMIC SUCCESS IN UNEXPECTED SCHOOLS

KARIN CHENOWETH | CHRISTINA THEOKAS

HARVARD EDUCATION PRESS
CAMBRIDGE, MASSACHUSETTS

Second Printing, 2012

Copyright © 2011 by the President and Fellows of Harvard College

All rights reserved. No part of this publication may be reproduced or transmitted in any form or by any means, electronic or mechanical, including photocopy, recording, or any information storage and retrieval systems, without permission in writing from the publisher.

Library of Congress Control Number 2011928653

Paperback ISBN 978-1-61250-101-7
Library Edition ISBN 978-1-61250-102-4

Published by Harvard Education Press,
an imprint of the Harvard Education Publishing Group

Harvard Education Press
8 Story Street
Cambridge, MA 02138

Cover Design: Sarah Henderson
Cover Photo: David De Lossy/Getty Images

The typefaces used in this book are Hoefler Text for body type and Univers Condensed for display.

Contents

Foreword

People familiar with primary and secondary schools in the United States tend to agree that nothing determines learning more than the quality of teaching, and that nothing determines the quality of teaching more than the quality of school leadership. Unfortunately, schools serving our least advantaged children are often in places where teaching and leadership leave much to be desired. Furthermore, pessimists assert that effective school leaders in hard-to-serve schools are endowed with rare skills and personalities that others cannot learn; that district-level bureaucracies make high performance in low-income communities all but impossible except in charter schools; and that poor children cannot excel unless we dramatically improve their home circumstances.

Certainly, there are grains of truth in pessimistic perspectives. Progress is difficult. But this optimistic book is full of hopeful examples. It profiles the exemplary principals who lead the "It's Being Done" schools that Karin Chenoweth explored in her two previous books, as well as a few additional principals that she and Christina Theokas discovered more recently. All of the schools have performed unusually well on standardized exams compared to schools serving similar students, and they rate well by other criteria as well.

The book heralds the possibility that by harvesting insights from successful practitioners, we could produce a new generation of professional development materials and experiences for leaders-in-training that might make a huge difference. The principals in the book serve elementary, middle, and high schools. Some of the schools are small, others are quite large. Almost all are regular public schools serving children of color growing up in poverty—the types of schools where poor performance is often seen as normal and that many people regard as lost causes.

Shifting racial, ethnic, and demographic patterns in the United Stages have made it almost cliché to point out that improving learning outcomes for children from less advantaged backgrounds is critically important to the nation's future. It is also common these days to recognize that schools seldom, if ever, improve without strong leadership. Our challenge as a society is to improve rapidly the quality of school leadership, especially but not exclusively by staffing schools with excellent principals.

It can be done. In this book, Chenoweth and Theokas suggest that highly effective principals are bright and relentless, but they are not superhuman. They provide enough detail to dispel much of the mystery about how these principals achieve exemplary results.

One of the more striking realizations that came to me upon completing the book is that none of the principals credited their effectiveness to any particular program of training. Of course, all are life-long learners who try to keep up with research, and they regularly participate in professional development activities for principals. But they credit their effectiveness mainly to their mentors, to what they learned in the classroom as effective teachers, and to the cooperation of other stakeholders that their own leadership helped cultivate. Their teaching experiences convinced them that children can perform at high levels when presented with high quality instruction. Their mentors taught them how to lead continuous-improvement schools where the adults are a community of learners who hold one another accountable for striving to excel.

The book reminds us that a number of research teams over the past decade have attempted to distill the features of highly effective school leadership. The second chapter reviews and summarizes several of the resulting ideas and frameworks. However, while such work is certainly valuable, it constitutes an incomplete curriculum for leadership training. In order to mimic the learning experiences that the principals in this volume seem to find most effective, we need more case teaching. In other words, we need written and video-graphic teaching materials based in realistic contexts that instructors can use to push principals-in-training to work through the types of challenges they will face on the job. In addition, because many principals have never seen highly effective schools, training should include visits to such schools if possible.

The chapters of this volume describe many of the challenges principals face and outline the attitudes and actions with which effective principals respond. There are a number of memorable phrases that capture the spirit of the work. For example, these principals are "relentlessly respectful and respectfully relentless." They monitor almost everything that matters, "inspecting what they expect." While they value high expectations for student achievement, these principals do not preach at teachers about high expectations and then wait for magic to happen. Instead, they push their faculties to achieve the norms and practices that teachers with high expectations manifest routinely. They "show instead of tell." As professional practices improve, expectations rise, because teachers learn that they and their students can achieve more than they previously believed.

Simply stated, these principals *are* relentless in finding ways to help their teachers learn to be better teachers. Sometimes they coach teachers based on the principal's own acquired expertise, but other times they import expertise from outside the school to fill gaps. One way or another, these principals make sure that their teachers have access to professional knowledge for improving their craft and that they put that knowledge to work in their own classrooms.

In education as in other fields, neither emotions nor intellect alone will suffice for achieving excellence; both hearts and minds are critically important. Principals of highly effective schools are thoughtful and specific about their conceptions of quality. They have high standards and strong opinions. They possess the courage to tell adults when the quality of the work needs to improve, the compassion and patience to provide supports to help others get better, and the audacity to replace poor performers who fail to make progress. Excellence in teaching and learning is the top priority, to which all others purposes are subordinate.

Getting It Done makes me more certain than ever that an important way forward for American education is to study what our best school leaders do and to use what we learn to improve professional development for current and future school principals. In this book, Chenoweth and Theokas show that there are indeed lessons to be harvested and passed along. Improving school leadership is an achievable goal that will advance both equity and excellence in the nation's educational outcomes. Let's get it done!

Ronald F. Ferguson
Faculty Director of the Achievement Gap
Initiative at Harvard University

Preface

I first began identifying schools with high-achieving children of color and children from low-income families seven years ago, when I began working at The Education Trust. Ed Trust is a national education advocacy organization that works to improve the academic achievement of all children, but particularly children of color and children from low-income families. My job was to find high performing and rapidly improving high-poverty and high-minority schools and write about what made them so successful. We knew they were out there and had something to share with the field.

Early on in my quest I visited a school in Boston where the principal, Mary Russo, had led a lot of improvement, and I remarked to her that many people believe that schools can't be expected to overcome the barriers of poverty and racial isolation. "They say this work can't be done," I said. She replied, "It's being done." I spent the next few years proving her right, and in her honor I began thinking of the schools I wrote about as "It's Being Done schools." These were schools that served large populations of students of color or students from low-income families or both with no entrance requirements—that is, for the most part they were just regular neighborhood public schools taking in whoever lived in their catchment area. No one would have been surprised if these schools had been low performing. But they were quite the opposite. Their students met or exceeded state standards at rates that put all of them at least in the ranks of ordinary middle-class white schools and put some of them at the top of their state.

These schools were doing something right, and it was my job to figure out what.

Over the years I found that although the schools shared many characteristics (see *It's Being Done: Academic Success in Unexpected Schools*, Harvard Education Press, 2007) and core practices (see *How It's Being Done: Urgent Lessons from Unexpected Schools*, Harvard Education Press, 2009), the most important constant among all of them was that they had highly effective leaders.

But that is too facile a conclusion. If leadership is key to the success of schools, what does that mean? Are highly successful leaders superheroes who drop in to save schools with a series of magic tricks only to disappear later? If so, we have no hope of helping all schools become high performing; we cannot expect an entire profession to be filled with magical superheroes.

When I talked with the principals, however, they didn't seem like superheroes. They seemed like—well, like principals. If you saw them at a conference of principals they wouldn't stand out. They don't stride through public spaces with the swagger of charisma and charm. Listening to them made running schools seem like more a matter of common sense than derring-do. And yet, judging from their results, what they were doing was clearly quite special.

When I was at their schools I would see teachers laugh at their quirks and argue with them over the best ways to do things. But those same teachers would conspiratorially corner me in hallways to whisper that the success of their school was all due to their principals. They would tell me stories of how their principals had helped them through the bad days and challenged them to improve on the good days; how their principals had created the atmosphere and the culture that allowed teachers to do the hard work of teaching and made teachers want to come to work every day. Anyone who has hung around schools much knows that that is not the way most teachers talk about their principals.

Clearly, I needed to write about leadership as a key element of school success, but I struggled with how to do so.

I thought about simply telling the stories of each of the school leaders and letting readers do the work of finding commonalities and differences. Chapter 1 of this book is an abbreviated version of what could have been an entire book describing highly effective leaders and their practices. Indeed, it could be argued that each of them deserves an entire book. But simply giving information about successful school leaders and their practices and successes seemed too easy and not particularly helpful. Current and aspiring principals—and those who supervise and train principals— need deeper analysis to help them think about whether successful leaders have something to offer the field of education or whether they should be dismissed as what some call freaks, flukes, and outliers.

On the other hand, the education field doesn't really need another academic study of leadership—there is plenty of good research establishing the importance of leadership and even the behaviors and characteristics of effective leaders.

It seemed to me that I needed to do something that combined storytelling and systematic research, and so I asked my colleague Christina Theokas, who is director of research at Ed Trust, to help me tell the stories of these school leaders in a systematic, methodologically rigorous way. A partnership was born. Together we agreed on a way to research the practices of effective leaders in a way that would put a human face on school leadership.

I bring long experience as a reporter and education writer; Christina brings long experience not only as an academic researcher but also as a practitioner who has worked at both school and district levels. She is as passionate about the obligation of schools to help students as she is about the obligation of researchers to provide rigorous, reliable analysis. Together we have created an unusual hybrid that I'm calling academically rigorous journalism or, perhaps, reportorial scholarship. We describe the methods we used in chapter 2, but in brief we have tried to hew to the best truth-telling traditions of both journalism and scholarship.

We hope readers find as much information and inspiration as we have found in these stories.

Karin Chenoweth
August, 2011

Acknowledgments

We are deeply grateful to the principals who allowed us to poke around their schools and their lives so that we and the rest of the field could learn from them. Their good humor and good sense help us understand that problems have solutions and there is joy and satisfaction in the work. Similarly, we want to thank the teachers, staff members, and students in their schools who helped us understand these leaders and the essential role they played in creating the highly successful schools we saw.

Marni Bromberg and Janelle Sands, our colleagues who assisted with data collection and analysis, brought not only their expert analytical sense but also their experience in classrooms to the work, helping us see patterns and commonalities among a very diverse group of people.

We are lucky to work with them at The Education Trust, a national education advocacy organization that, under the leadership of Kati Haycock, has helped the country understand that what schools do matters deeply not only to individual students but to our nation as a whole. As this generation struggles to create a "more perfect union," this lesson is ever more important.

Great thanks are due to Kati and to Ed Trust's Richard Lemons and Judy Karasik for their valuable suggestions on how to improve this manuscript. Daria Hall's work early on helped shape the criteria that were used to evaluate schools, and her team continues to identify inspiring schools. In fact, all our colleagues at Ed Trust, through their interest and questions, helped enrich our work.

We further want to acknowledge Doug Clayton and Jeff Perkins at Harvard Education Press for believing in this book. Marcy Barnes, Daniel Simon, and others whose names we don't know worked quickly and efficiently to publish it faster than we thought was possible.

Finally, we want to thank our families and friends, who had to live with our obsession about school leadership for more than a year. Special thanks go to Charlie, David, Emily, and Rachel.

Introduction

Many longtime educators and quite a few academics scoff at the notion that schools can be expected to educate all children as utopian and unrealistic. They point to the continued low achievement of huge swaths of student populations (most notably children of low-income families and children of color) as proof that schools can't be expected to educate all children to a shared standard, no matter how much politicians hector and harangue.

But some educators have demonstrated what it takes to make the dream of high achievement for all children a reality—not only do they embrace the mission, they have developed the knowledge and skills required. They are the school leaders of highly successful schools that serve large populations of students of color and students from low-income families. This book is an attempt to learn from thirty-three such leaders. We set out to understand how successful principals, as the leaders of their schools, improve educational practices and learning for all students. What characteristics, behaviors, goals, and practices are shared among the principals? What differences exist and why?

They were identified through their schools—all of them high performing or rapidly improving with large populations of children of color or children from low-income families. These schools are flying high—and much like flocks of birds, they fly farther and faster because of their tightly knit collaboration and ability to keep focused on a distant goal.

The criteria used to identify the schools are spelled out in detail in *It's Being Done: Academic Success in Unexpected Schools,* but in general they are schools that most people would consider challenging, and their academic achievement results unexpected.

1

Chapter 1 describes each of the leaders who are included in the study. As readers will see, they span a wide range of experience and external characteristics, and their schools range in size, level, and locale. In chapter 2, we review what the existing research literature on school leadership says and the way we conducted this study.

We begin sharing our findings in chapter 3. In it, we discuss what kinds of backgrounds and beliefs this group of highly successful school leaders bring to the job. They share many commonalities with other principals around the country. And yet what they do and how they do it—how they guide instruction (chapter 4), manage basic managerial functions (chapter 5), and create a climate and culture in their buildings (chapter 6)—helps their schools be more successful than most. Chapter 7 is a concise discussion of what kinds of relationships the principals have with those outside their schools—in particular their district offices and community service providers. These findings are interesting and tantalizing and point to more work that should probably be undertaken about the kinds of help and support principals need from their district offices—and too often don't get.

Finally, in the conclusion, we try to bring together all the elements that we separated out in the previous chapters to describe what we can learn from highly successful principals. Some say that a few successful school leaders don't prove anything. Just as we cannot expect every baseball player to have a .350 batting average, we can't expect every principal to lead a school that successfully overcomes the disadvantages of the students. But most baseball players study the way .350 batters stand and swing in order to improve their own batting. They may never achieve .350 that way, but they might achieve .300. And the fact is that far too many of our schools aren't batting anywhere near .300.

This book attempts to study a group of .350 batters—and even a few .400 batters—with the understanding that if we replicated these school leaders all over the country, we could solve many of our educational problems. Since we can't magically do so, it is incumbent upon the rest of us to try to learn from them what we can. It is in that spirit that we have written this book.

CHAPTER ONE

Why Should We Listen to These Guys?

It's Being Done school leaders are a skeptical bunch, and for good reason. Nonsense dressed up in important-sounding jargon so plagues the field of education that skepticism is an important survival tool of competent people.

This chapter acknowledges what we assume will be the healthy skepticism of our readers by briefly describing the thirty-three school leaders who participated in this study.

First off, we want to make clear that we do not pretend to have included every excellent school leader in the country. Many more outstanding school leaders exist—in fact, we've run into a few since we finished our data collection and had to exercise great discipline not to reopen the process to include them.

The principals we have included, however, have demonstrated track records, many under very difficult circumstances, which makes them very special and worthy of study. Some of their schools were profiled in two previous books, *It's Being Done: Academic Success in Unexpected Schools and How It's Being Done: Urgent Lessons from Unexpected Schools.* Others are more recent discoveries. For some of their schools, we have included charts with the student achievement trends. Data for the remaining schools can be found on their respective state department of education Web sites. Some charts tell more dramatic stories than others, but they all demonstrate impressive results in schools with large percentages of students of color or students from low-income families. We start with the elemen-

3

tary school leaders, then the middle school, and finally the high school leaders. The names of those who are part of the study are italicized upon first mention.

ELEMENTARY

Let's start with *Barbara Adderley*. Adderley was a veteran teacher and administrator when she arrived at M. Hall Stanton Elementary in North Philadelphia, a school that was profiled in *It's Being Done* (see table 1.1). A graduate of Cheyney State and Arcadia University, she was a veteran special education teacher and then a staff developer and facilitator when she arrived at Stanton in 2001 as principal. The part of North Philadelphia in which the school sits looked like a war zone when she arrived. From the school's asphalt playground could be seen two little candy stores and what seemed like acres of plywood covering the windows of the low-rise apartment houses and row houses that surrounded the school.

The school—a huge, hulking, three-story brick building still heated with a coal furnace—was dirty and dangerous, plagued by what teachers called the "third- and fourth-grade gang wars." One fifth-grade teacher, Christina Taylor, remembered years later that her students would beg to be allowed to stay in her third-floor room all day rather than go to the cafeteria where they would be in danger.

Not surprisingly, there wasn't much learning going on. It was one of the lowest-performing schools in Philadelphia, making it one of the lowest-performing schools in the state.

Adderley was careful to identify those teachers who were good teachers and those who needed additional help and support to be good teachers. She quickly made Christina Taylor her math coach and Kathleen Shallow her literacy coach, two roles she considered essential in helping teachers improve their instruction.

By the time Adderley left, students at Stanton met or exceeded standards at percentages at or above the rates posted by students in Pennsylvania in most grades and subjects (see figures 1.1 and 1.2). The kids had not changed in those years—they were just about all African American and all

Table 1.1: M. Hall Stanton Elementary, Philadelphia, Pennsylvania

Principal: Barbara Adderley, 2001–2007
Grades PK–7
476 students
98% African American
99% Low-income

Source: Common Core of Data, public school data, 2009–2010, http://nces.ed.gov/ccd.

came from low-income families. And yet they were meeting state reading and math standards at rates similar to schools serving white middle-class students. This was an extraordinary achievement on the part of Adderley, who left in 2007 to return to her hometown, Washington, D.C., to be a regional superintendent.

In one of the tragedies of urban education, the next principal systematically undid just about everything Adderley had put in place. Many of the staff members whom Adderley had so carefully trained to focus on educating each individual child left, including Christina Taylor and Kathleen Shallow, who became principal and literacy coach, respectively, of Eisenhower Middle School in Norristown, Pennsylvania, which has posted significant student gains since their arrival. Stanton fell back into chaos and low performance within a remarkably short time.

It is tempting to read into that little history that it's all about the individual principal; to think that leading high-poverty, high-minority schools is a job for superhumans with extraordinary powers. This is the Principal-as-Hero story line that has long clouded the real issues of school leadership. Certainly, Barbara Adderley was an extraordinary principal—but she is the first to say she's no superwoman. She put into place policies, procedures, and processes that marshaled the efforts of the entire staff at Stanton in ways that helped all the children. That description makes her sound more like a bureaucrat than a leader, yet she is neither a superwoman nor a bureaucrat but a supremely competent educator steeped in her craft who knows what it takes to provide children with a real education.

Figure 1.1: Grade 5 reading, Pennsylvania System of School Assessment, M. Hall Stanton Elementary School

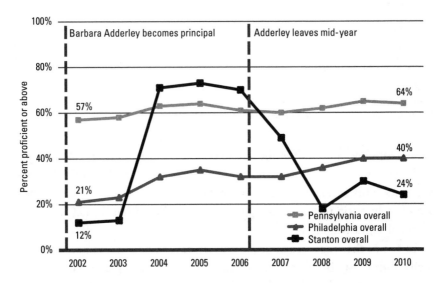

Source: Pennsylvania Department of Education, 2002–2010.

In subsequent chapters we will explore what we mean by "policies, procedures, and processes." But now we want to introduce you to the others in our study sample.

Like Adderley, *Molly Bensinger-Lacy* was a veteran educator when she arrived at Graham Road Elementary in Fairfax, Virginia (see table 1.2). A graduate of the University of Texas–Austin, she began her professional life as a music teacher in Texas and later taught English in Turkey. When she moved back to the States she began teaching in Delaware, where she met her husband. After earning a degree in linguistics, she and her husband both took teaching jobs and eventually became principals in Fairfax County, Virginia, a large suburban district just outside of Washington, D.C.

Immediately before becoming principal at Graham Road, Bensinger-Lacy spent five years as principal of an elementary school where she led improvement. But she longed for an even bigger challenge. She has a deep commitment to the idea that public schools provide the entry point to

Figure 1.2: Grade 5 math, Pennsylvania System of School Assessment, M. Hall Stanton Elementary School

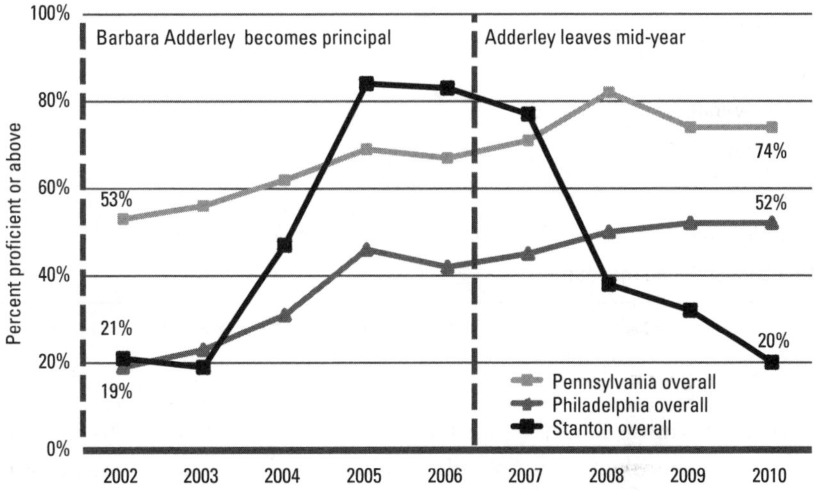

Source: Pennsylvania Department of Education, 2002–2010.

opportunities for poor children and children of color, and was convinced that schools could do a better job by such children.

With thirty-five years' experience in education, she applied for the job as principal of Graham Road Elementary. Graham Road, which is profiled in *How It's Being Done,* sits on the border between two neighborhoods. Across the road is a neighborhood of single-family homes. Behind is a large townhouse complex that has attracted many low-income families who have recently immigrated from Central America, the Caribbean, Africa, Southeast Asia, and elsewhere. As the school filled with their children, the students from the single-family houses drifted away into private and magnet schools and, by 2004, very few middle-class children remained. Eighty percent of the children qualified for free and reduced-price meals, a measure of poverty and, by Bensinger-Lacy's calculations, about 85 percent of the children spoke a language other than English at home. Achievement had fallen through the years, and Graham Road was the

Table 1.2: Graham Road Elementary School, Falls Church, Virginia

Principal: Molly Bensinger-Lacy, 2004–2010
Grades PK–6
406 students
88% Low-income
69% Latino
13% Asian
10% African American
45% English language learner

Source: Common Core of Data, public school data, 2009–2010, Fairfax County Public Schools, http://nces.ed.gov/ccd.

lowest performing school in the county. Some in the county thought the school was so broken that it should be closed and the students dispersed.

Bensinger-Lacy took on the challenge in 2004, and by the time she left, in December 2009, Graham Road was one of the highest-performing schools in the state, with most students not only meeting but exceeding state standards at rates that far exceeded some of what Bensinger-Lacy called the "country club schools" in her county (see figures 1.3 and 1.4).

Bensinger-Lacy is the first to say that it was the teachers at Graham Road who were responsible for the improvement. What *she* did was organize the school in such a way that the teachers were able to be successful, including making sure that teachers were able to learn from master teachers. One of those master teachers, *Aileen Flaherty,* eventually became her assistant principal, and because of her centrally important role in the improvement of Graham Road, she is one of the assistant principals we have also included in this study.

Mary Haynes-Smith encountered one of the most difficult situations faced by any American educator: her school, city, and home were devastated by Hurricane Katrina. With her school completely destroyed, she was asked to become principal of nearby Mary McLeod Bethune Elementary school in Orleans Parish. It wasn't in much better shape. "The building was deplorable. Dead rats, feces, dirty clothes. The cafeteria was the pits. The ceilings were on the floor. The concrete was buckled, the desks were shabby, the books were stinking. I don't know how anyone expected us to go in there. But the district said the community needed a school in order to survive. They came in and painted and put up new sheetrock. But little did they know that the termites would come right behind them."

That first year, the school enrolled any student who could make their way there. "It was open to every student in the city," she said. "We had children who hadn't been in school for six months," including many juvenile delinquents. "We forgot that if they had ankle bracelets on they had done armed robberies. We had no suspensions. There was no better place for them to be." In those early days, she said, "We were in survival mode. Everybody was poor and had lost everything."

From Smith's long history as a teacher and principal in New Orleans, she knew the teaching force and was able to bring the best teachers from her old school as well as select the best from Bethune and from around the city. She then spent time building a new culture of collaboration among the disparate staffs. "My main goal was to build a team and get them to buy into the vision I had that this would be the best school."

In the intervening years Bethune has settled into serving its immediate neighborhood, which is characterized by poverty and a high crime rate. Smith and her teachers are sure to be gone by nightfall and even in daylight walk each other to their cars. Just about every one of the students comes from a low-income family and almost all are African American. In addition, the students and their families are constantly dogged by the emotional and economic difficulties of living in a part of the city that has yet to recover from near-destruction. "We are their mothers, their fathers, their grandparents, their teachers, their cooks, their laundromat—we have to be everything," said Smith, who had a washing machine and dryer installed in the building so no child would have to wear dirty clothes at school.

Despite the challenges faced by the students, all of Bethune's sixth-graders met state reading standards in 2009, compared with 70 percent of sixth-graders in the state; 62 percent of Bethune's sixth-graders exceeded standards, compared with only 4 percent of sixth-graders in the state.

Figure 1.3: Grade 5 reading, Virginia Standards of Learning, Graham Road Elementary School

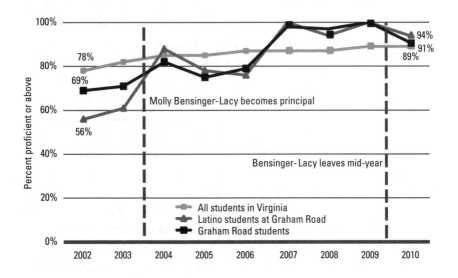

Source: Virginia Department of Education, 2002–2010.

Smith remains unsatisfied. For her, basic and even advanced proficiency "is not a high bar." The principal wants her students to not only pass state tests but have the opportunities that most middle-class students take for granted—to graduate from high school with postsecondary choices such as college and meaningful work. To reach those goals, the children of Bethune must learn to read well, master a lot of content, and be able to demonstrate their knowledge on tests and elsewhere. To make sure that happens, Smith tells her teachers to "teach these children as if they were your own."

In her fifteenth year as principal, Smith says the job is still "a joy" and adds, "I love my children, I love my staff, and hopefully I can make a difference in the lives of my children, my staff, and my parents."

Terri Tomlinson and *Debbie Bolden* arrived together at George Hall Elementary School in Mobile, Alabama, at a particularly low point in its history. George Hall sits in a low-income neighborhood known as

Figure 1.4: Grade 5 math, Virginia Standards of Learning, Graham Road Elementary School

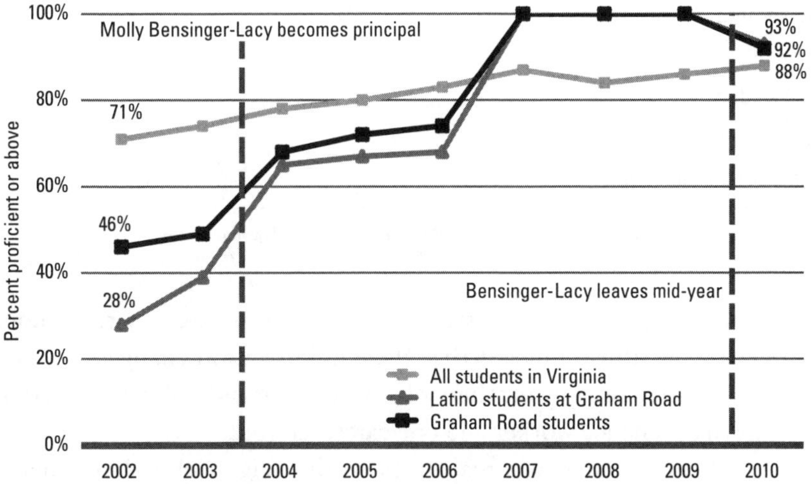

Source: Virginia Department of Education, 2002–2010.

Maysville, which is home to small single-family homes and nearby federal housing projects of the kind that were built in the South—small, low, and without many features to distinguish them from warehouses (see table 1.3). George Hall was one of the lowest-performing schools in the city, and the state had started making noises about taking it over if it didn't improve. To give a sense of how low performing it was, the fifth-grade students on average were reading at the 24th percentile on the SAT-10, a nationally norm-referenced test given to students in Alabama. This put them well below where African American students in Alabama scored—which, in turn, was significantly below the scores of white students in Alabama.

Tomlinson and Bolden had been principal and assistant principal, respectively, of a low-income school where they had presided over gains in student achievement, but in looking back they realize that that school had been well led for decades and was fully functional when they arrived. At George Hall, they were entering a completely broken school, and they had

Table 1.3: George Hall Elementary School, Mobile, Alabama

Principal: Terri Tomlinson, 2004–present

Assistant Principal: Debbie Bolden

Grades PK–5

549 students

99% Low-income

99% African American

Source: Common Core of Data, public school data, 2009–2010, http://nces.ed.gov/ccd.

been tapped as part of a reconstitution process instituted by the school district. Reconstitution meant that the administration changed and the entire staff had to reapply for their jobs. Tomlinson and Bolden hired back only one maintenance worker and one cafeteria worker.

Reconstitution came as a real shock to the neighborhood, and many parents and community members were deeply upset. Teachers who had been local institutions—who had taught many of the parents and even many of their parents—were no longer at the school. It is sometimes easy to dismiss the deep attachment people feel toward their unsuccessful neighborhood schools. But change is always disquieting, and even unsuccessful schools are sometimes the most functional institutions in an impoverished neighborhood like Maysville, which was known throughout the city for its drug trade, daytime prostitution, and nightly shootings.

This is the environment Tomlinson and Bolden walked into, and when they looked back from a few years' distance, admitted that they might not have gone if they had realized how bad the situation would be. They never wavered in their belief that the students would be successful if "the right structures were put in place," as Tomlinson put it, but the deep and entrenched neighborhood hostility was formidable.

To begin with, departing staff trashed the building, which meant that the first thing Tomlinson and Bolden had to do was hire a dumpster and start hauling trash. The two of them, with the maintenance worker they had rehired, spent the summer cleaning the building and installing some of the basic equipment like bulletin boards at the same time they were hiring a new staff, writing the school handbook, laying out policies and procedures, and trying to quiet parental and neighborhood fears.

As an example of the kind of welcome they had from the neighborhood, a dead cat was left on the rooftop air conditioner, fouling the air in the building, and the back of the building was "fished," meaning that dead fish were rubbed on the bricks, causing a stench that could only be eradicated with a power washer.

Some days, they said, they would work all day and then not even be able to speak to each other as they left the building. They would exchange exhausted looks and get into their cars to drive home to rest up for the next day.

Providing a new physical environment was, they felt, extremely important. They wanted children and their parents to feel that things were going to be different from the moment they walked in on the first day of school. They also wanted to ensure that teachers felt that the school was a supportive, not hostile, environment. "We didn't let the teachers come until we cleaned it up," Bolden said. "It was unbelievable." Because Tomlinson had spent the previous decades working in the Mobile School District, she knew who the best teachers were, and she recruited from all over the city. Teachers who otherwise wouldn't consider teaching at George Hall agreed to come because they wanted to work with her.

In addition to hiring the best teachers they could find, Tomlinson and Bolden were determined to change the tone of the building. Children and parents who were used to being yelled at—and who gave as good as they got—were spoken to quietly and respectfully. They installed a washing machine and dryer so that children would always be able to wear clean clothes.

A mark of how immediately successful they were in providing a different environment comes from Cathy Gassenheimer, with the nonprofit school-reform organization A+ Alabama, who had regularly visited the school in the previous few years. She said that when she visited that fall, she asked, "Are these the same children?" They were the same children but looked cared for and happy instead of neglected and beaten down.

By 2007, the students at George Hall were performing at national norms, and in 2010 they were, on average, reading at the 71st percentile

Figure 1.5: Grade 5 reading, Stanford Achievement Test, 10th edition, George Hall Elementary School

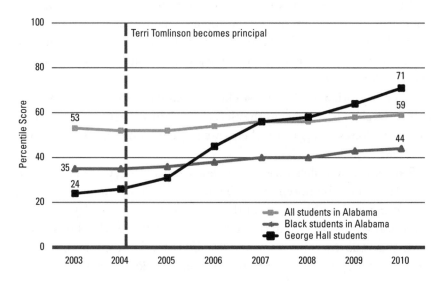

Source: Alabama Department of Education, 2003–2010.

and performing at the 94th percentile in math on the SAT-10—exceeding the performance of many wealthy, white students around the country (see figures 1.5 and 1.6).

Tomlinson has said that she is too near retirement to take on another turnaround project like George Hall, but Bolden left George Hall to take the principalship of another low performing school in Mobile. The first year of her principalship, the school made Adequate Yearly Progress, which is the primary accountability measure of the federal No Child Left Behind law, and all signs point to the school continuing its improvement in her second year. Her contributions to George Hall's improvement would have been sufficient to be included in this study, but her ability to show improvement in another school puts Bolden in a special category all her own.

Few stories are as dramatic as George Hall's, but Ware Elementary comes close. Ware Elementary, which was profiled in *How It's Being Done,* is a regular public school that sits on the army base at Fort Riley,

Figure 1.6: Grade 5 math, Stanford Achievement Test, 10th edition,
George Hall Elementary School

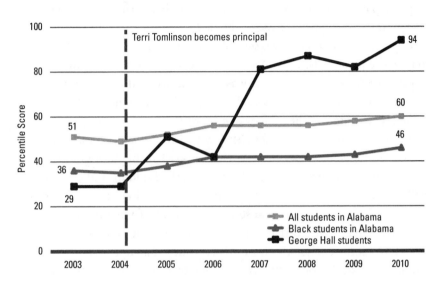

Source: Alabama Department of Education, 2003–2010.

Kansas. Fort Riley is the major training base for the U.S. Army infantry, and it is home to five elementary schools and one middle school. Ware serves the children of enlisted troops, most of whom tend to be young and very mobile. As a result, it has a very high mobility rate, usually hovering around 50 percent.

It would be easy to say that schools which serve the children of military families have it easy—soldiers, after all, are required to attend parent conferences, and a work ethic and discipline can be assumed. And yet Ware Elementary was one of the first schools in Kansas to be classified as needing improvement in July 2001 because of its low performance. Not only was academic achievement low—only 59 percent of the fifth-graders met state reading standards, for example—but morale was low, marked by a series of union grievances, and discipline was a serious problem, as testified to by the high number of student suspensions in the previous couple of years.

Deb Gustafson was a veteran administrator who had held just about every job there is in a school, including school secretary, custodian, and teacher. As principal she had led marked improvement in another school in the district, and to avoid going to Ware she had taken on a second school. After three years as principal of two schools, the superintendent asked her again to take the principalship of Ware and this time didn't allow Gustafson to refuse. Gustafson's first action was to sit down and cry—she knew the school's reputation as a broken school and knew that she wouldn't be welcomed by the staff. When she walked into the building that July, she was hit with the stench of urine, a mark of what she saw as a "broken school."

Like Tomlinson and Bolden, Gustafson—with the help of her daughter—spent the summer personally cleaning the building and painting the walls as well as hiring a new head of maintenance. In part because of low staff morale and in part because of the nature of teaching on an army base, Ware had high staff turnover, and Gustafson had to immediately hire eleven new teachers, a chore she considered an opportunity to begin molding the staff around her vision. One of the key hires she made was *Jennie Black*, a special education teacher with whom she had worked in a previous school. Black, the wife of an enlisted army soldier, was returning to Fort Riley after having been posted in Georgia for a few years. Black became Gustafson's right-hand person, and the two formed a team just as powerful as Tomlinson and Bolden were at George Hall, which is why not only Gustafson but also Black is included in this study.

During the first year of Gustafson's principalship, her focus was on establishing a different school culture and a different context for teachers in terms of how work was organized, and scores made a jump. After that, the focus was on improving instruction, and the test scores took another jump and have since stayed at levels that make it one of the top-performing schools in the state, with just about every student meeting standards and many students exceeding standards. While serving as principal, she has taken on the work of helping other principals around the state, something she could do because Black is fully capable of running the school.

Another story of an educator who took a school from dysfunction to high performance is *Sharon Brittingham,* former principal of Frankford Elementary School in Frankford, Delaware, which is profiled in *It's Being Done*.

A longtime middle school teacher and assistant principal, Brittingham arrived at Frankford in 1997 after the school had been put under federal supervision for its violation of civil rights laws. The Office of Civil Rights had found that the school over-identified African American students—particularly boys—as needing special education services and then segregated them away from the general education population.

When Brittingham arrived, she found a staff that didn't expect much of the students, most of whom were low-income and either African American or Latino. The most common phrase among the teachers was, "You can't make chicken salad from chicken shit," a particularly redolent phrase in that school because many of the parents worked in the poultry industry that dominates that area of Delaware. Brittingham told the teachers, "If you don't believe all kids can learn, what are you here for?" But, she said, as important as teachers' beliefs about the ability of children to learn are their beliefs about their ability to teach. She focused her energies on helping teachers improve their instruction, bringing in high-quality help from the district and state. "We brought in the Delaware Reading Project, the Delaware Writing Project . . . people to help teachers teach phonics," she remembered later. She also helped teachers become more comfortable with the idea of "inclusive" classrooms, meaning classrooms that included students with disabilities, sometimes co-taught by a general educator and a special educator.

Test scores soared, and when Brittingham retired in 2006 to work with principals around the state with the University of Delaware, she left a school that was near the top of the state, posting proficiency rates of 100 percent in some grades and some subjects. One of Sharon Brittingham's most important mentors was Principal *Gary Brittingham* of nearby East Millsboro Elementary School, who, surprisingly enough, is not related to her. About half the students at East Millsboro are from low-income families, about one-fifth African American and 15 percent Latino, making East Millsboro, which is profiled in *It's Being Done,* a more diverse school than Frankford. But just about every group performs at high levels. Gary Brittingham led the school for almost thirty years, during which it was always relatively successful. But, he said, when the school developed professional learning communities focused on improving instruction, it improved markedly, and when he left in 2008 it was one of the top-performing schools in the state. "I expected 100 percent of my students to achieve at a high level and made every effort to provide whatever it took to get them there. This was communicated at every open house, every faculty meeting and every newsletter. It was posted in the school for all to see and believe. We did not look at students by income or race. We looked at the data and determined what they would need to achieve and provided it."

He left East Millsboro in the hands of his longtime assistant principal, Mary Bixler, who has maintained student achievement at high levels. He is now working at the district level as assistant superintendent.

Another principal who left to work at the district level as assistant superintendent is *Arelis Diaz*. Born in Chicago to recent immigrants from the Dominican Republic, her health caused her parents to move to Puerto Rico so that she could be in a warmer climate. When she was nine they moved back to the mainland U.S., this time to Massachusetts, where her father worked in a factory. After attending Calvin College, Diaz became a teacher of English as a Second Language (ESL) at North Godwin Elementary School just outside of Grand Rapids, Michigan. About 40 percent of North Godwin's students are Latino, 35 percent white, 20 percent African American, and 80 percent from low-income families. Many of the students are recent immigrants, including a sizeable population from Bosnia, Vietnam, and Central and South America. As an ESL teacher, Diaz began a program that brought large numbers of family members into the school to learn English, computer skills, and become actively engaged in their children's education by learning literacy skills with them.

When Diaz became principal in 2001, she said, she inherited a staff that for the most part did not know each other, were not used to working together, and were demoralized by the demographic shifts in the population from a mostly working-class and middle-class school to one characterized by unemployment and poverty. By the time she left in 2005 to become assistant superintendent of the district, North Godwin was performing at levels similar to much wealthier schools in Michigan. Diaz took a job with the Kellogg Foundation in 2010, determined to spread the practices she instituted at North Godwin to other schools.

Dolores Cisneros-Emerson is another daughter of immigrants. She is a native of Brownsville, Texas, where her parents came to from Mexico. Brownsville, all the way in southern Texas, had until recently a border so porous that Texans would go to Mexico to get their hair cut and Mexicans would go to Texas to go to the dentist. The drug war that has raged through the area has cut down severely on the easy come-and-go across the border, but just about everyone in Brownsville seems to have ties to Mexico and speaks Spanish. Cisneros-Emerson remembers being very disengaged as a student, not particularly liking to read and often lagging behind her peers. It wasn't until college that she woke up to the need to work hard, and as a teacher and administrator she is sympathetic to children who don't learn the first time they are taught. "You have to keep trying, even if it takes sixteen times," she said. After years as a teacher and then assistant principal, she applied for the principalship of Morningside Elementary, just a mile from the border where just about all the students are Hispanic, more than half are limited English speakers, and almost all come from low-income families.

The school was labeled "academically acceptable" in the Texas ranking system, which Cisneros-Emerson calls "unacceptable," and when she arrived in 2006, she told the staff that she expected that at least 90 percent of the students would meet or exceed standards. "An entire grade level [of teachers] told me, 'We have never gotten 90 percent, why should you expect it?'" Flabbergasted that teachers would openly say that they didn't expect their students to meet standards, Cisneros-Emerson began making public among her teachers scores on the state tests and the benchmark tests so they could see that the students of some teachers did better than others. This began the process of using data as a tool to improve and individualize student instruction. That first year the school improved its scores by about 10 percent, and the following year was named as "recognized" by the state, and from 2007 on it has been "exemplary" in recognition of the fact that more than 95 percent of the school's students met or exceeded state standards, compared to 72 percent of students in the state. Cisneros-Emerson credits her district, Brownsville ISD, for having provided strong support as well as a cohort of principals she could rely on for help and moral support.

Natalie Elder is another principal who relied on strong ties with her district and other principals in Chattanooga, Tennessee, as she helped her school, Hardy Elementary, improve. In 2000 the new Tennessee standardized test scores were used to rank all the schools in the state from best to worst. Dominating the lower part of the list, with nine of the "worst" twenty schools in the state, was Chattanooga. Hardy was at the bottom. That list gave an impetus to the district, the local Public Education Fund, and a local foundation, the Benwood Foundation, to do something radical to improve its schools. The nine schools, including Hardy, became the focus of what was called the "Benwood Initiative," which is described in *It's Being Done,* and which involved intense training and support of the principals and assistant principals.

Hardy's students were almost all poor and African American, mostly living in nearby housing projects, near where Elder herself grew up. A veteran science and math teacher and, later, assistant principal at three different schools in Hamilton County, she was excited to come back to the school in her childhood neighborhood. She found a disheartened staff that needed to be convinced that educating all children is possible. "I use myself as an example because I came from poverty," she said, adding that she would sometimes take her teachers for walks among the housing projects to let them understand where the children came from. "Your environment shouldn't dictate your ability to learn. Your ability to learn depends on teachers that challenge and engage you." After Hardy was named the most improved school in the state, Elder was named one of the most effective principals in the state. She left Hardy in 2009 and took a job in the district office of Stamford, Connecticut.

No principal in our study speaks more highly of her district than *Melinda Young,* former principal of Wells Elementary School in Steubenville, Ohio, which was profiled in *How It's Being Done*. A native of Steubenville, Young is a graduate of the local Catholic high school and the local Franciscan University, which trains many of the teachers for the district. She initially became a Title I reading teacher and, after a stint in the central office, became principal of Wells Elementary in 2000, confident she could do the job. "[I was] really excited because I wanted to be with the students and teachers. In the central office, you feel really closed off from the schools."

Under Young's leadership, Wells was the highest-performing school in Steubenville, but Young has always been careful to point out that, despite its economic implosion as a rustbelt city, Steubenville's schools—particularly at the elementary level—have gotten stronger. Steubenville's teachers and principals alike attribute that to a well-implemented and enthusiastically embraced Success for All program, adopted by the district in 2000, Young's first year as principal of Wells.

Success for All, a program developed at Johns Hopkins University and implemented in more than one thousand mostly high-poverty schools, has been denigrated as a "scripted" program. But teachers in Steubenville say that, although it provides a lot of structure, it permits a great deal of flexibility for teachers to adapt it and teach to their personalities. Its careful data systems and materials mean, however, that students throughout the district find a consistency of instruction that is particularly important as their families move in search of better housing options. "Prior to this system, teachers all did what they wanted to do," Young said. "You may think you have a better way, but consistency is the better way."

Certainly Wells showed great consistency, often posting 100 percent proficiency rates in reading, math, and even sometimes in science and social studies with an integrated student body—about 60 percent of the students came from low-income homes, 30 percent were African American, and another 16 percent identified as "multiracial." In 2010, after shepherding the school's move to the first floor of the new high school building, Young took a job in the central office as program director, where she helped apply for the district's federal "Race to the Top" grant of more than $600,000.

Sheri Shirley became principal of Arkansas's Oakland Heights Elementary, profiled in *It's Being Done,* in 2001 when it was a low performing school. A longtime teacher fresh from a master's program in school administration and with a mentor principal who helped her through the early days, she said that her first goal was to keep the school from falling under sanctions for failing to meet student achievement targets.

With about 80 percent of the students meeting the qualifications for free and reduced-price meals and about 30 percent students of color—mostly Latino—Shirley describes the families in the school as "working poor," with many parents involved in the poultry and food-processing industries.

"That first year I was there, our scores rose 40 percentage points," she said recently. "When we received our scores, our fourth-grade teachers were worried the district was going to think we cheated. I had to tell them that the district would think we were teaching."

Before her arrival, teachers had never been given test scores to analyze, and Shirley gave them time and training to help them with data analysis. "We did a lot of standards alignment and backwards planning so that teachers would know what they needed to do to get their kids ready for the next grade," she said, adding that her goals have shifted now that 80 percent of students are proficient every year. "Now our goals target the 20 percent of struggling learners. Now we look at interventions instead of basic curriculum. A new goal that we look at is making sure we are challenging our brightest students in a differentiated classroom."

Cynthia Kuhlman retired several years ago from Atlanta Public Schools after a full career as a teacher, district office personnel director, and, finally, principal of Centennial Place Elementary School, which is profiled in *It's Being Done*. The school was part of a complete change for the neighborhood that was part of the federal Hope VI program to redevelop blighted public housing projects. It involved tearing down the oldest public housing projects in the country, replacing them with a mixture of rented and owned townhouses and single-family homes. Centennial Place was built to replace the old school, and Kuhlman was encouraged to apply for the principalship, a job, she says, she was "confident" she could do well.

She had been struck by the fact that despite the school's proximity to the Georgia Institute of Technology, no student from the neighborhood had ever been admitted. She was determined that her school would open that kind of opportunity to its students, most of whom came from low-income families and most of whom were African American, and tried to hire teachers who shared that vision. "I really tried to confirm every candidate's commitment to a belief that poor minority children are limited only by our ability or failure to provide opportunities for them," she said recently. The curriculum developed by the faculty, under Kuhlman's supervision, was organized around science themes with enrichment from the arts. Students' performance on state assessments put Centennial Place among the top schools in the state.

Since her retirement, Kuhlman has been working with a local foundation and has served on the board of the Charles Drew Charter School. She reports that three former Centennial Place students attended Georgia Tech during the 2010–2011 school year.

All the previous stories are of veteran educators who were steeped in the professional literature and knowledge of instruction before they took the job of principal. *Von Sheppard* has a different background, but a similarly dramatic story to tell. One of the most highly recruited football players ever to emerge from Minnesota, he played wingback for the University of Nebraska, a fact that makes college football fans sit up and take notice. He signed with the Minnesota Vikings, but an injury cut short his football career, which he finished up playing in Europe. When he left professional football, he returned to Minnesota and took a job as football coach at a St. Paul high school and worked in student affairs at the University of St. Thomas in St. Paul, Minnesota. After three years he took a job as a high school assistant principal, a job usually associated with discipline.

When his superintendent asked, he agreed to lead a school that was widely acknowledged to be the worst in St. Paul, Dayton's Bluff Achievement Plus Elementary School, profiled in *It's Being Done*. From one point of view, he was an obvious choice for the job—an imposing physical presence, he was not intimidated by the out-of-control behavior on the part of both students and parents, who had been used to being able to walk into classrooms to yell at teachers and even hit children whom they had thought had harmed their sons and daughters. Some of the parents were themselves rather scary—they were part of the drug gangs that helped make that part of St. Paul the most dangerous in the city. And, Sheppard said, that part of the city "had the highest concentration of sex offenders in the Twin Cities."

If all that was needed was a calming disciplinary presence, Sheppard fit the bill. But from another point of view, he was a less obvious choice. With little experience dealing with young children, he admits he didn't know how to relate to them—he was used to teenagers, not kindergarteners who rushed to hug his knees. In addition, he knew little about instruction. But he was determined to demonstrate to the world that poor children and children of color could achieve at high levels.

Under an agreement with the teachers' union, the district required all teachers to reapply for their jobs, which were restructured to require additional hours, devoted to collaboration. Only about one-third were hired back. The rest of the staff was recruited from around the city. Sheppard arrived after the staff had been assembled, and he knew they would be wary of someone with his background. He straightforwardly told them that "we would go on a journey together" to learn about instruction. At the same time, he enrolled in a principal-development program at the University of Pittsburgh under Lauren Resnick to develop his knowledge and skill as an instructional leader.

Together, he and the staff made Dayton's Bluff a school that, from its data, looked like a regular middle-class school in Minnesota. But it wasn't—almost all of its students were from low-income families, and in addition to its 46 percent of African American students, 26 percent were Hmong, a refugee community from the mountains of Laos whose members have often done very badly in American schools.

After Sheppard left in 2005 to take a job in Minneapolis, the school was combined with another nearby school. The combined students and faculty took a while to recover, but several years later the school was once again posting proficiency rates that put it in the "regular Minnesota school" category.

Sheppard is currently assistant superintendent in the Office of School Leadership of Boulder Valley School District in Colorado.

Tom Graham is another principal with an atypical background. His first career was as a Marine fighter pilot, and when he retired he became a teacher, rising to principal after just a few years.

When Graham arrived at Griegos Elementary in 2002, he found a school that, by his account and that of several teachers, had been well led for a long time by the previous principal. It was a comfortable neighborhood school in a working-class neighborhood of Albuquerque where about three-quarters of the students are Hispanic and about 60 percent come from low-income families. Never particularly high achieving in the past, it is now one of the top-performing schools in New Mexico. For example, 90 percent of the students met state reading standards in 2009, compared to 58 percent in the rest of the state.

Nothing Graham or the teachers say indicates that the improvement over the past few years has been dramatic. Rather, as the state standards were put in place, the school heightened its focus on what students needed to learn. When Graham arrived he found that a small group of teachers had been working together, and they were among the more successful teachers in the school. "I just opened the door to more participants," Graham said, requiring that there be a common curriculum throughout the school. As federal and state accountability mechanisms took hold, teachers realized that they needed to identify students who needed extra help and thought deeply about how to provide that help.

Graham also brought an old-fashioned attitude to citizenship. Every student and adult in the building is expected to adhere to the "Griegos Way," summed up in the school motto, "Do the right thing at the right time." Graham said recently that he chose that motto because, "It is simple, powerful, and easy to understand."

Students who misbehave often have to weed the yard or go on "trash patrol" with Graham, who has a military dedication to tidy surroundings and becomes visibly upset when he encounters an unswept entryway, much less litter in the hallway. The retired major also brings a military sense of discipline to the question of attendance. A second absence often means Graham's appearance at the student's home, his visit emphasizing to parents the importance of sending their children to school.

ELEMENTARY–MIDDLE SCHOOL

An example of a successful transfer of leadership comes from *Elain Thompson* and *Valarie Lewis* of P.S./M.S. 124 in Queens, which is profiled in *How It's Being Done*. Thompson began her career as a para-educator in Queens, New York, and took advantage of a program that had been worked out between the United Federation of Teachers and the school board to finish college and get her certification as a teacher. After teaching for fifteen years she became an assistant principal at P.S. 124 in Queens, where about 90 percent of the students qualify for free lunch and most students are either African American or Latino, with a sizable population of children recently immigrated from India and Pakistan. When she began, she said, she was handed a "big bunch of keys," but none of the keys opened anything, something she said demonstrates that "there were no expectations of the job." She said her principal expected just as little of the students and teachers, and in fact spent much of her time running a private religious school on the side.

Valarie Lewis, first a substitute teacher and later a permanent teacher, had returned to the classroom after years of staying home with her young children. Lewis and Thompson enjoy relating how tense and difficult their initial relationship was. "I annoyed her," Lewis says about Thompson because she was always questioning why things were run the way they were.

When the principal left, Thompson took on the principalship, and she and Lewis together convinced the teaching staff to adopt Core Knowledge as the school's curriculum. Lewis applied for a grant to pay for the training and materials, and the entire staff took on the project of teaching the curriculum that was developed by E. D. Hirsch to ensure that all children—particularly children who live in poverty—have the foundation of knowledge and skills that educated people take for granted. It is a rich and complex program that often requires teachers to increase their own knowledge and skills, and P.S. 124 took it on wholeheartedly.

Test scores soared. Lewis became assistant principal and turned down offers to be principal at two other schools so that she could stay at P.S. 124. The way New York school politics worked, however, she knew she wouldn't be able to turn down another principalship. Thompson wasn't ready to retire, but in order to ensure that Lewis be her successor, she retired early rather than see Lewis go to another school. Although P.S. 124 was successful, she said, she thought its success still too fragile to entrust to someone not steeped in the school's culture. After retiring she did consulting work for the Core Knowledge Foundation but kept in frequent touch and often stopped by the school and even volunteered regularly.

Meanwhile, the parents of the school noticed that students who were doing wonderfully at P.S. 124 floundered when they went to the neighborhood middle school. "They were bored," Lewis said, adding that when she visited the middle school she saw that the level of instruction was below what her students were used to.

For that reason, the parents lobbied that P.S. 124 expand to be a middle school. The district agreed, and the school added grades six, seven, and eight, which is why it is now P.S./M.S.(for middle school) 124. It has test scores that put it comfortably among some of the most affluent schools in New York City despite the fact that it is has one of the higher poverty rates of any school in the city.

MIDDLE SCHOOLS

Roxbury Prep Charter School in Boston, which is described in *How It's Being Done*, is another story of school leaders working to continue a culture of excellence (see table 1.4). The only charter school leaders in this study, *Will Austin* and *Dana Lehman* both came into an existing school and continued practices and policies that had been previously established.

Austin and Lehman each carry the title of co-director and divide the job into two distinct responsibilities: Austin is responsible for managing the building, budgeting, recruitment, relationships with the school's board, and fund-raising. Lehman was, until the 2010–11 school year, responsible for curriculum and instruction, including the hiring and supervision of teachers. However, Lehman said, she wouldn't hire someone without Austin's agreement, and he wouldn't develop a budget without consulting her. Austin came to the job after a two-year stint at Steppingstone, a nonprofit urban education organization, after graduating from Harvard College, whereas Lehman had more traditional training for the classroom at Swarthmore College, followed by teaching physics at both a private and public high school. She began at Roxbury Prep as a science teacher and after three years in the classroom was surprised to be tapped to became co-director. "Internally, I knew I could do it, but I was definitely overwhelmed and started to immediately feel responsible for ensuring the school remained a success."

That was the fifth year of Roxbury Prep's existence, and it was already one of the top-performing middle schools in the state (see figures 1.7 and

Table 1.4: Roxbury Preparatory Charter School, Roxbury, Massachusetts

Coprincipals: Will Austin (2002–present) and Dana Lehman (2004–2010)

Grades 6–8

246 students

72% Low-income

62% African American

37% Latino

Source: Common Core of Data, public school data, 2009–2010, http://nces.ed.gov/ccd.

1.8). During the 2010–11 school year Lehman joined Uncommon Schools, which is the charter school network to which Roxbury Prep belongs, and she was succeeded by Amy Zaffuto, who had been a teacher at the school, thus continuing the cultivation of leadership from within.

Port Chester Middle School's *Carmen Macchia* is another example of a leader who led growth in his school and then left the school in the hands of his former assistant principal. Port Chester, which was profiled in *It's Being Done,* is in a working-class town in Westchester County, just north of New York City, that has long been home to recent immigrants—first German, then Irish, then Italian, and now Latino. When Macchia was hired as principal of the low performing middle school in 1993, teachers were wary of yet another principal who talked big and might be gone soon. To demonstrate his commitment, he promised teachers he would stay five years. He ended up staying seventeen.

The son of immigrants from Italy, Macchia had a fellow-feeling for the students, most of whom were newly immigrated from Central and South America. "I was the first Macchia to graduate from college," he said, in an acknowledgment of the low expectations many educators had for Italian American students when he was young.

The first couple of years of his principalship were "all law and order," Macchia said, making sure the school was clean, orderly, and students no longer feared what would happen if they used the bathrooms. The results from the first administration of the New York State standards-based tests in 1999 proved shocking to Macchia and the school. Only about one-third

Figure 1.7: Grade 7 reading, Massachusetts Comprehensive Assessment System, Roxbury Preparatory Charter School

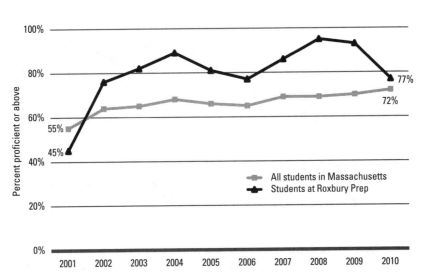

Source: Massachusetts Department of Education, 2002–2010.

of the students met state reading and math standards. The then-superintendent went to each of the schools in the district to say that if this were a business he would close it, which proved even more shocking to the teachers and staff than the results themselves.

Patrick Swift, who arrived that year as assistant principal from a school in the South Bronx, said that he "walked into fury." But Macchia began a process of focusing teachers on questions of what students needed to learn, which students were not doing well, and which teachers were more successful with which students on which topics. At the same time, he brought in nationally known professional developers who could help teachers think about how to improve instruction. Test scores soared, and Port Chester, with about 65 percent of the students meeting the qualifications for free and reduced-price lunch and about 75 percent Latino, began looking like an ordinary middle-class school in the state.

In 2010 Macchia retired, leaving the school in the hands of Swift, his longtime assistant principal, who said he was hoping to reenergize the staff

Figure 1.8: Grade 8 math, Massachusetts Comprehensive Assessment System, Roxbury Preparatory Charter School

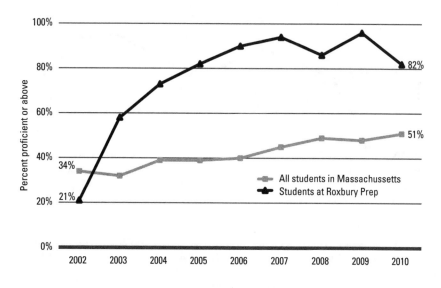

Source: Massachusetts Department of Education, 2002–2010.

and refocus on the kinds of things that gained the school a National Blue Ribbon Award under Macchia. "We do not need to reinvent the wheel, we just need to put some air in the tires," he said.

Across the country in Texas, *Susan Brooks* led Lockhart Junior High School, which was profiled in *How It's Being Done,* to recognition as an exemplary school—meaning, in Texas parlance, that more than 90 percent of students pass all the state assessments given in reading, math, science, and social studies—much higher percentages than the rest of the state. Lockhart, which serves a huge geographical area ranging from the town of Lockhart (south of Austin) to ranches and rural areas across more than three hundred square miles, serves a student body where 55 percent of its students are Latino and a similar percentage come from families with low incomes.

Brooks grew up in coastal Texas where her father had a shrimp-packing business. After attending Southwest Texas State University, she taught speech, drama, and history before becoming an administrator, spending a few years as a superintendent before returning to schools in the 1990s. In 1997 she came to Lockhart as assistant principal and became principal a year later, where she established the idea that the school was in the "rescue business. We rescue a lot of kids." After ten years as principal, Brooks retired and won a seat on the Lockhart School Board.

MIDDLE–HIGH SCHOOLS

Diane Scricca was an experienced teacher and administrator who grew up in Queens and was steeped in what she describes as demanding and high-quality teacher and administrator training in New York City. She took the job as principal of Elmont Memorial Junior-Senior High School in 1990 and stayed for almost thirteen years. Home of the Belmont Racetrack, Elmont is immediately east of Queens in Long Island's Nassau County. New York has no publicly available data from back then, but Scricca says that the junior-senior high school, which was profiled in *It's Being Done,* was mediocre "at best" back then with a graduation rate around 80 percent. Its white students, who comprised about 40 percent of the population, were doing better than its African American and Latino students, who were about 45 percent of the student population, but even few of the white students earned Regents degrees—the college preparatory degree in New York State. Almost none of the African American students did.

A large school with almost two thousand students in grades 7–12, by 1995 the school was recognized by *Redbook* magazine as one of the best high schools in the state. Scricca focused closely on improving classroom instruction with a careful system of classroom observation that continues to this day. Every untenured teacher is observed at least seven times a year and every tenured teacher is observed at least twice a year, the idea being to help teachers develop from novices concentrating on classroom management and lesson planning to experts who need to improve the quality of their assignments and questioning techniques. "The process was one of support where we went into classrooms to see how we could help teachers reflect on their instructional decisions so they could improve their performance," said Scricca.

In one of Scricca's treasured yearbooks from her years as principal is a letter from a teacher remembering her anticipation of her first observation from the "demanding Diane Scricca."

> When the day finally arrived, my heart was racing so fast I could hardly breathe, much less read and teach to a class of not-too-motivated ninth-graders. Miraculously I survived and was soon surprised to discover that I had passed her test. OHMYGOSH! This fifty-year-old fledgling teacher might make it after all. Next came a gentle question, "And what do you think you might have done to make this an even better lesson?" she asked. And so began my journey to learn the craft of teaching and establish a career I came to love.

Scricca hired only those teachers who shared her expectation that all students would be successful in high school and go on to be successful in college. The interview question she became known for was, "Are you going to love my kids?" One of her successful hires was social studies teacher *John Capozzi*. Capozzi, who also grew up in Queens, worked for a furrier company immediately out of college and lived in Hong Kong buying and shipping furs for many years. But he had always wanted to be a teacher, and his clear passion for helping students learn history earned him a chance at Elmont.

In his second year, Scricca assigned him to teach eleventh-grade Regents History along with two other second-year teachers, a key subject that was usually taught by experienced teachers. "Experience got us 63 percent passing rates," she said drily. "I believed that these teachers were going to do better just as I expected them to believe that their students would do better," she said years later. "We ended with 93 percent passing and 63 percent mastery" that year, she said, referring to an advanced level on the state Regents exam.

Capozzi later became chair of the social studies department and then an assistant principal. When Scricca left to take a central-office job in a nearby district, another of her assistant principals, Al Harper, became principal of Elmont. After two years he left to become superintendent for the Elmont Union Free School District, and Capozzi became principal.

Under Capozzi, Elmont has continued to do what he calls "move the rock slowly." With graduation rates that hover in the high 90 percents, every year he has aimed at improving the number of students who receive not just the academic Regents Diploma (just about all Elmont students do that) but a Regents Diploma with an Advanced Designation, representing a more rigorous course of study. In 2010, 49 percent of graduates earned that, up from 40 percent two years before. Just to give one comparison: only around 60 percent of African American and Latino students in the state even graduate.

Scricca, who subsequently became superintendent of Riverhead School District and is now assistant professor at Mercy College, said recently: "John has done for that school what I couldn't do," to which Capozzi replied, "No, I called her every single day." Even six years into his principalship, Capozzi still continues to bounce ideas off Scricca and credits her with providing crucial mentoring during his early years. She, in turn, refers to Elmont as "the love of my life" and pointedly questions Capozzi every time the graduation rate falls a percentage point or two from the 99 percent she left it with.

University Park Campus School, profiled in *It's Being Done,* is also on its third leader, but it has a different kind of history, one that began with neighborhood deterioration. Clark University sits in a hard-luck neighborhood of Worcester, Massachusetts, and when the neighborhood looked so downtrodden that it was losing some prospective students, university officials decided to reengage with its city. It spent money repairing many of the nearby homes, but officials realized that as long as children were unsuccessful in the neighborhood school, there would be a constant outflow of families.

Together with Worcester Public Schools, Clark founded a new school, University Park Campus School, led by Donna Rodrigues, who recruited *June Eressy* as her English teacher and, somewhat later, history teacher *Ricci Hall.* Eressy had been a longtime English teacher at another Worcester high school and was convinced that students could do better if their schools were organized to serve them better.

Originally housed on the campus of the university, University Park Campus School later moved a few blocks away to an old, creaky schoolhouse with big, drafty windows and wooden floors. Today the school houses 230 students in grades 7–12, almost 80 percent of whom come from low-income families and 65 percent of whom do not have English as their first language. To attend, students must live within a few blocks of the school, but the neighborhood—dominated by the triple-decker houses typical of that part of New England—produces more children than there is space in the school. As a result, the school holds a lottery among students whose parents have provided their contact information and indicated an interest in enrolling their child.

When the students arrive, they are typically reading below the fifth-grade reading level. For years Eressy was the person who met with them during the special summer session the school has for new students. She assessed their reading, diagnosed their problems, and made plans to accelerate their achievement. Even after Rodrigues left to work with Jobs for the Future and Eressy became principal, she continued to meet individually with incoming students so that she would have a clear idea of where students were and where they needed to be.

Through the years University Park has consistently been one of the highest performing schools in the state, with almost every student graduating and going on to college. After many years of high performance, Eressy took on the principalship of a nearby low performing school in addition to University Park. During the next three years, Ricci Hall, who had been hired as a teacher straight out of Clark University's urban teacher preparation program, became the de facto assistant principal, and when Eressy took a job in the district office, he became principal. "I felt it was time to give Ricci a chance," she said. In the 2010–2011 school year she took the principalship of a "turnaround" elementary school, Chandler Elementary in Worcester. One of the lowest performing schools in the state of Massachusetts (fewer than 15 percent of third-grade students met state reading and math standards in 2010), Eressy was given three years to show significant improvement and make Adequate Yearly Progress, a measure of federal accountability. After talking with each teacher in the school, she asked the district to transfer only two of the teachers who would be unable, in her opinion, to embrace the idea of helping all students achieve.

"I don't believe in just getting rid of teachers," she said. "You can help them get better."

In the spring of 2011, Eressy said she thought Chandler would show significant improvement on the state's spring assessments "because of all the supports" she put in place, including training for teachers in building a positive culture and climate, literacy, and math, as well as the afterschool programs and individual tutoring for students.

Of Eressy, Hall said, "She was a great mentor teacher and mentor principal." He is carefully preparing one of his teachers to take on more leadership responsibilities, much the same way that Eressy prepared him by giving him increasingly complex tasks.

HIGH SCHOOLS

Another leader in this study who emerged from the world of sports is *Ricardo Esparza*, who went to Central Washington State University on a wrestling scholarship. When he graduated and became a math and physical education teacher, he also worked as a high school wrestling coach and, later, assistant principal in Grandview, Washington. When the opportunity to lead his own school came up, he took it, applying for the job of Granger High School principal.

Granger High School, which is profiled in *It's Being Done*, sits in the Yakima Valley, a large agricultural valley across the Cascade Mountains from Seattle. The town itself is small, and most of the adults—and many of the children—work in the fields picking hops, cherries, apples, and other crops. This was familiar territory for Esparza, whose family, originally from Texas, migrated with the crops until he was in first grade, when his parents settled in the Yakima Valley. Granger High School is high-poverty, with 90 percent of the students qualifying for free and reduced-price meals. Few of the students' parents graduated from high school, and when Esparza walked up on his first day, he found the school's sign tagged with gang graffiti. Gangs are a forceful presence in the Yakima Valley, and throughout his time at Granger, Esparza continually struggled to keep students from being sucked into them.

Only about 40 percent of adults in the town have graduated from high school, according to U.S. Census data, and when Esparza arrived in 2001, he says the graduation rate was somewhere between 30 and 40 percent. This is difficult to pinpoint exactly because the state doesn't report graduation rates before 2002. Within one year of Esparza's arrival, the graduation rate was close to the state's rate of 66 percent, and thereafter graduation rates have been higher than the state rate. Along with the soaring graduation rates were steadily improving reading and writing proficiency rates on the tenth-grade test all Washington students take. Although those improvements were never mirrored by math and science results, meaning that Granger could never have been considered high achieving, the improvement posted by Granger in the years between 2001 and 2008 is so dramatic as to be remarkable.

After he left Granger, Esparza moved to Colorado and married a fellow principal. He took the principalship of an official "turnaround" school just outside of Denver—that is, a school designated by the state as being in the lowest 5 percent of schools. Fort Logan Elementary, which has three grades, from third through fifth, was characterized by poor behavior and low morale. Within a few months of his arrival, Esparza had energized the staff, many of whom said they would not have lasted even a few months if he had not been there, and got student behavior under control. The manuscript for this book had to be completed before the first round of state tests were reported.

Esparza recently wrote a book about his experience at Granger, *Breaking the Poverty Barrier: Changing Student Lives with Passion and Perseverance*.

Another high school leader who led enormous growth in her school is *Lisa Tabarez,* the former principal of Imperial High School, which is profiled in *How It's Being Done* (see table 1.5). Tabarez is herself from California's Imperial Valley—a desert that has been turned into farmland through an extensive irrigation system. The daughter of a bill collector and a teacher's aide, she participated in Talent Search, a federal college-going program, and returned to the valley as an English teacher after attending the University of Redlands. In 2000 Barbara Layaye, who had been Tabarez's high school physical education teacher and was then superintendent of the Imperial School District, recruited her as assistant principal of

Table 1.5: Imperial High School, Imperial Beach, California

Principal: Lisa Tabarez (2003–2010)
Grades 9–12
924 students
35% Low-income
74% Latino
29% English language learner

Source: Common Core of Data, public school data, 2009–2010, California Department of Education, http://nces.ed.gov/ccd.

Imperial High School. After three years Tabarez became principal, and in 2010 replaced Layaye as superintendent.

Imperial is not a high-poverty school the way Granger is—only about 40 percent of the students qualify for free and reduced-price meals. With a Latino student population of 70 percent, it is, however, the kind of working-class school that is not expected to be an academic powerhouse. There was a complacency about being one of the top schools in the valley, Layaye remembered years later. One way Tabarez helped her staff understand the need to help each student meet standards was by taking all the faculty members to the gym and telling them each needed to make a basket. When some faculty members objected that they were shorter than others and had less athletic talent, she agreed but said they still needed to make a basket. Staff members described that as a crystallizing moment in understanding that each student needed to meet standards, even if they didn't yet have the skill or ability. "Meeting the standards is important," Tabarez said. While she was principal, Imperial went from being in the bottom third of the state to being in the top third of the state in terms of academic achievement (see figure 1.9). It graduated just about all its students and sent nearly all its graduates to either a two- or a four-year college, where they needed remediation much less often than most California students.

Conrad Lopes, a longtime teacher and assistant principal, had an opportunity that many principals dream of: he got to open his own school.

Figure 1.9: California Academic Performand Index, Imperial High School

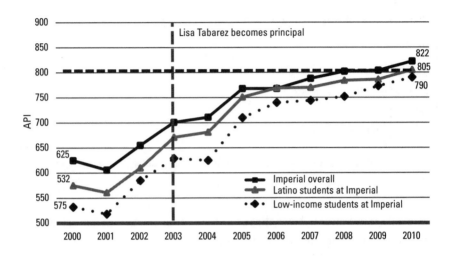

Note: The dashed line at 800 indicates California's API goal for all schools.

Source: California Department of Education, 2000–2010.

Tapped in 2000 by the Fayetteville, North Carolina, school district to begin Jack Britt High School, he was able to hire every teacher and staff member. He began the school with the goal of making sure that every student would be successful. "We want to prepare students for college, the workforce, whatever they choose to do after high school," he said years later. "We don't want them to say, 'I'm going to community college because I can't get into a four-year college.'" He brought several teachers and administrators with him from his previous school, Seventy-First High School, including longtime geometry teacher *Denise Garison,* whom he began to groom for an administrative position. In 2002 she became assistant principal and was given responsibility for increasingly complex tasks as a way to prepare her for the principalship, including budgeting and scheduling, as well as participating in hiring and helping teachers improve instruction.

When Lopes retired in 2009, he became principal of a high school in South Carolina, and Garison applied for and was appointed principal of

Jack Britt. "My goal when I was hired as principal was to maintain the culture of the school," Garison said. Key to that culture: "Understanding that we as teachers must expect the best out of each child who comes through our doors."

For many years it was difficult to tell whether Jack Britt's academic achievement was much different from most North Carolina high schools. However, in the last few years North Carolina has improved its reporting on graduation and has instituted new end-of-course (EOC) exams. It turns out that Jack Britt is one of the top-performing schools in the state. With an integrated student body—about half the students are white and half are students of color, mostly African American—a higher percentage of Jack Britt's students meet the standards when compared to most other schools in the state. To take Algebra I as an example, more than 95 percent of white and Latino students at Jack Britt pass the exam, and 92 percent of African American students pass. Statewide, 86 percent of white students pass, whereas 73 percent of Latino students and 63 percent of African American students pass. At Jack Britt, 92 percent of low-income students pass, while statewide 68 percent of low-income students pass. In other words, where the state has enormous and discouraging achievement gaps, Jack Britt High School has small ones that in some cases have dwindled to virtual nonexistence.

One gap makes Jack Britt stand out: its white students graduate at a higher rate (83 percent) than the state's white students as a whole, but its African American students graduate at an even higher rate (92 percent). Garison's goal is to improve both rates so that "Our graduation rate [is] at 100 percent, our EOC's scores at 100 percent."

These thirty-three principals and assistant principals completed at least parts one and three of our survey instruments, which were at the heart of this study (see table 1.6). We want to acknowledge another five who completed the first part of the survey but for whatever reason—sometimes ill health, sometimes lack of time—could not complete the second and third parts of our survey and so are not included in the study sample. By filling out the first survey, they added to our knowledge of the initial preparation and goals they brought to the job, and we greatly appreciate that. The five are: Mary Bixler, principal of East Millsboro Elementary School in Delaware; Fran Castillo and Hazel Cruz of P.S. 83 in Manhattan, Christina Taylor, principal of Eisenhower Middle School in Pennsylvania (formerly at M. Hall Stanton Elementary School); and Teri Wagner, principal of Lapwai Elementary in Idaho.

Principals are among the busiest people we know, and we will always be grateful that the thirty-three principals in our study sample were able to carve out the time to be part of this study.

CONCLUSION

As is clear in the individual portraits, the principals who participated in this study fit no particular mold. In subsequent chapters, however, it will become clear that what they do share is a belief in the power of schools and education to improve the lives of children, a belief in the power of principals to improve schools, and a willingness to do what it takes to exercise that power.

Table 1.6: Principal names and schools

Principal name	School name	City	State
Barbara Adderley	M. Hall Stanton Elementary School	Philadelphia	PA
William Austin	Roxbury Preparatory Charter School	Roxbury	MA
Molly Bensinger-Lacy	Graham Road Elementary School	Falls Church	VA
Jennie Black	Ware Elementary School	Fort Riley	KS
Debbie Bolden	George Hall Elementary School	Mobile	AL
Gary Brittingham	East Millsboro Elementary School	East Millsboro	DE
Sharon Brittingham	Frankford Elementary School	Frankford	DE
Susan Brooks	Lockhart Junior High School	Lockhart	TX
John Capozzi	Elmont Memorial Junior-Senior High School	Elmont	NY
Dolores Cisneros-Emerson	Morningside Elementary	Brownsville	TX
Arelis Diaz	North Godwin Elementary School	Wyoming	MI
Natalie Elder	Hardy Elementary School	Chattanooga	TN
June Eressy	University Park Campus School	Worcester	MA
Richard Esparza	Granger High School	Granger	WA
Aileen Flaherty	Graham Road Elementary School	Falls Church	VA
Denise Garison	Jack Britt High School	Fayetteville	NC
Tom Graham	Griegos Elementary School	Albuquerque	NM
Deb Gustafson	Ware Elementary School	Fort Riley	KS
Ricci Hall	University Park Campus School	Worcester	MA
Mary Haynes-Smith	Mary McLeod Bethune Elementary School	New Orleans	LA
Cynthia Kuhlman	Centennial Place Elementary School	Atlanta	GA
Dana Lehman	Roxbury Preparatory Charter School	Roxbury	MA
Valarie Lewis	P.S./M.S. 124 (Osmond A. Church)	Queens	NY
Conrad Lopes	Jack Britt High School	Fayetteville	NC
Carmen Macchia	Port Chester Middle School	Port Chester	NY
Diane Scricca	Elmont Memorial Junior-Senior High School	Elmont	NY
Von Sheppard	Dayton's Bluff Achievement Plus Elementary School	St. Paul	MN
Sheri Shirley	Oakland Heights Elementary School	Russellville	AR
Patrick Swift	Port Chester Middle School	Port Chester	NY
Lisa Tabarez	Imperial High School	Imperial	CA
Elain Thompson	P.S./M.S. 124 (Osmond A. Church)	Queens	NY
Agnes Terri Tomlinson	George Hall Elementary School	Mobile	AL
Melinda Young	Wells Elementary School	Steubenville	OH

CHAPTER TWO

So, What Do We Know About Principals and School Leadership?

Given that the premise of this book is that principals have a considerable impact on student success, in this chapter we wanted to review some of the evidence that supports this claim and some of the outstanding questions and controversies about the job of principal that remain in the field. We pose five key questions and review the research available to answer them in addition to foreshadowing the findings from the research with the It's Being Done principals. The research broadly frames how the role is understood, expectations and standards for principals, and possible high-leverage practices, activities, and behaviors. Following this, we describe in detail our research, which aims to explain the specific practice and choices of principals we believe — and their school data suggest — have accomplished both excellence and equity in their schools. We are not attempting to test a theory or quantify an effect size for a particular practice. Instead, we are trying to learn from principals who have done the hard work of improving schools and to distill lessons that may be useful to other practitioners. The lessons, in the following chapters, are organized around core responsibilities the research has identified; instructional, managerial, cultural, and external relations.

Bradley Portin, of the University of Washington, makes the point that we often look at what principals "might" do and think this is what they "should" do.[1] Indeed, research on the job of principal has explicated a long and detailed list of tasks, responsibilities, and potential styles for principals to adopt. Our research tries to answer a rather straightforward question: How do principals with a record of improvement and success for all students manage all that the role entails?

WHAT KIND OF SCHOOL LEADERS DO WE NEED?

It seems intuitive that a school principal exerts a significant influence on the student achievement in her building. Given this—and the decades of research on leadership generally and school leadership specifically—we might expect the field and practice of principals to be clearly articulated, with aligned training and evaluation. Instead, however, we find intensive scrutiny of the job and different visions for how the job should be done, as well as a long and overwhelming list of responsibilities for one person to accomplish.[2] Lynn Beck and Joseph Murphy observe that the metaphors of school leadership have changed frequently over the years; no sooner have school leaders assimilated one recommended approach than they are seemingly urged to move in a different direction.[3] Principals have been asked to be bureaucratic executives, humanistic facilitators, instructional leaders, and most recently transformational leaders. These various roles reflect the changing demands of school principals, with job descriptions getting more complex and longer as additional skills needed to be successful are incorporated yet none taken off the list.

Indeed, the job itself has changed, particularly in conjunction with standards-based reform. With schools and school systems being held accountable for their contributions to student learning, a redefinition of leadership necessarily follows.[4] No longer can principals just be managers, keeping their constituents happy and tamping down problems as they arise. They must drive improvement, and to do this they must understand curriculum and instruction and rethink school processes to better meet the identified needs of students, a description that loosely fits the model of instructional leadership.[5] This change, however, can entail increasing the commitments and capacities of school staff, involving components of what is called transformational leadership.[6] Some scholars have thus argued for "integrated leadership," which combines both instructional and transformational leadership.[7]

With new demands for better-trained high school graduates and the expectation that *all* students achieve the same outcomes, yet another conception of leadership has emerged: distributed leadership. The idea of distributed leadership is partly an answer to the suggestion that only superheroes could actually do the job and a rejection of the flawed idea that just working harder or more will achieve the desired ends.

At its simplest, distributed leadership means that the principal's duties are shared among other administrators or teachers. Richard Elmore goes beyond simply reshuffling assignments and calls for a fundamental shift in organizational thinking that redefines leadership as the responsibility of everyone in the school.[8] The principal's role is to guide, rather than control and manage, every aspect of what goes on in the classroom. This reflects the reality that no matter how deep a principal's understanding of instruction, only classroom teachers have the day-to-day knowledge of specific students in specific classroom settings and ought to be able to make instructional choices. The role of leadership is to create unity around a shared vision and common tasks; it is not about micromanaging instruction.

These different frames for leadership are not mutually exclusive, although they are often treated as such in the research, and there are even more descriptors of leaders including moral, participative, and strategic. The principals documented in this study, on the whole, perceive their role in a way consistent with the instructional leadership frame. But that doesn't fully capture it. Elements of transformational and distributed leadership also clearly shine through at different points in their tenure and reflect both their individual leadership styles and the particular needs of the school they lead. Ultimately, these are sophisticated leaders doggedly trying to increase student achievement, and it is difficult to characterize them in a single way.

WHAT IS SCHOOL LEADERSHIP?

The leadership styles just discussed can mask what the job of principal is all about and can inadvertently lead to the belief that school leaders all need to be cut from the same mold. In reality, what much of the research indicates is that effective leaders, in schools and other fields, are best characterized through a specific set of practices. This next section describes the essential actions of leaders, as seen from research in education and from the professional field. There have been numerous articulations of these practices, and the field has not always agreed on the work of principals. Yet it appears that research is beginning to cohere around some central actions—core ideas that will frame the chapters to follow.

Kenneth Leithwood and colleagues, after reviewing all the literature, tried to simplify the practice of principals and defined three core responsibilities essential to successful student learning:

1. Setting Direction
2. Developing People
3. Developing the Organization[9]

Each of these broad categories comprises three to five specific practices. For example, Setting Direction includes: building a shared vision, fostering the acceptance of group goals, creating high performance expectations, and communicating the direction.[10] Others within education have also attempted to classify leadership practices and have come to similar conclusions. For example, Hallinger and Heck describe the practices of instructional leadership as "purposes," "people," and "structures and social systems," whereas Conger and Kanungo include "visioning strategies," "efficacy-building strategies," and "context-changing strategies."[11] James Collins and Jerry Porras in their study of visionary companies came to similar conclusions about leadership and leaders, suggesting that their work was all about influencing groups of people toward achievement of goals, attracting dedicated people, and playing key roles in guiding their companies through crucial times and barriers.[12]

Richard Elmore describes a similar list of core practices. However, he explicitly describes the activities in relation to one another and in service of instructional improvement. In this way, his work differs from literature on management and leaders in business and other industries. He describes teaching and learning as a "knowledge-intensive" enterprise. The three practices above are described similarly, but he focuses on instruction:

(1) enhancing the skills and knowledge of people in the organization, (2) creating a common culture of expectations around the use of those skills and knowledge, and (3) holding the various pieces of the organization together in a productive relationship with one another. Still, he adds a fourth practice to this list: holding individuals accountable. Accountability is essential in his model of leadership; he asserts everyone has a contribution to the collective result of schooling, and part of the role of the leader is to manage and account for everyone's contribution.

These articulations of what principals should do can seem deceptively simple. Yet in practice they can prove extremely difficult to realize, especially when principals are saddled with myriad responsibilities that pull the day-to-day focus from instructional improvement to managing operations. And still, setting a direction, developing people, and developing organizations broadly frame the mechanisms through which principals influence student learning. And that is no less the case for the principals in this study, who explored these three areas of leadership as they described their own practice. Chapter 3 will discuss how these principals developed a vision, and chapters 4, 5, and 6 will provide examples of exactly how they developed their staffs and schools to achieve their vision.

In addition to explicating leadership generally, a number of educational groups and organizations have specified what principals ought to know and be able to do. As standards have been developed to describe what students ought to know and be able to do, standards have been created for the leaders who are in charge of this learning. These lists attempt to draw from the growing research and describe characteristics of *good* school leaders. Most encompass the three basic practices described by Leithwood and colleagues, but many go beyond, suggesting high-leverage activities, dispositions, and performances. These views are more nuanced and raise the bar on how leaders do their job. It is not enough to have a vision; principals must establish this vision around high expectations for both student and staff learning.

The National Policy Board for Educational Administration (NPBEA), in 1990 and then again in 1993, was the first to attempt to organize a platform for practice, finding one conspicuously missing from the field.[13] The essential skills and knowledge encompass twenty-one domains, organized under four broad themes, and blend the traditional content-driven curricular knowledge with leadership, management, and process skills (see table 2.1). The purpose was to broadly define the foundation blocks for the preparation of school principals. As such, it is extensive and tries to represent both the subject content and techniques of leaders.

The two key associations that represent principals also created guides for principal performance. Instead of all the detail contained in the knowledge and skill base that demonstrates the complexity of the position, they chose to emphasize standards. For example, the National Association of Elementary School Principals (NAESP) created a guide, *Leading Learning Communities: NAESP Standards for What Principals Should Know and Be Able to Do*. Their belief is that charisma and good management skills are not sufficient to be successful in the position, so they specified quality standards for performance. The six standards are:

1. Lead schools in a way that places student and adult learning at the center.
2. Set high expectations for the performance of all students and adults.
3. Demand content and instruction that ensure student achievement of agreed upon academic standards.
4. Create a culture of continuous learning for adults tied to student learning and other school goals.
5. Use multiple sources of data as diagnostic tools to assess, identify, and apply instructional improvement.
6. Actively engage the community to create shared responsibility for student and school success.[14]

Similarly, the National Association of Secondary School Principals (NASSP) specifies seven areas of professional development for principals to improve their practice.[15] The ideas are quite similar to the standards for elementary principals in that they both emphasize that schools are centers for learning and that this ought to be the core work of the principal. In addition, they highlight some essential tools to support the work, including the use of data and collaboration. The seven areas are:

Table 2.1: The knowledge and skill base necessary for leaders

Functional domains	Programmatic domains	Interpersonal domains	Contextual domains
Leadership	Instruction	Motivating others	Cultural values
Information collection	Curriculum design	Interpersonal sensitivity	Legal and regulatory applications
Problem analysis	Student guidance and development	Oral expression	Public relations
Organizational oversight	Measurement and evaluation	Written expression	Policy and political influences
Judgment	Staff development		
Implementation	Resource allocation		
Delegation			

Source: Scott Thomson, *Principals for Our Changing Schools: The Knowledge and Skill Base* (Fairfax, VA: National Policy Board for Educational Administration, 1993).

1. Validate teaching and learning as the central activities of the school.
2. Engage with peers and teachers in career-long learning to improve student achievement.
3. Collaborate with colleagues to achieve organizational goals while still meeting the needs of individuals.
4. Use data in planning and decision making for continuous development.
5. Model effective teaching and learning processes.
6. Incorporate measures of accountability that direct attention to valued learning outcomes.
7. Find opportunities to work, discuss, and solve problems with peers.

Finally, the Chief State School Officers (CCSO) and the National Policy Board for Educational Administration (NPBEA) created the Interstate

School Leaders Licensure Consortium (ISLLC) and defined new Standards for School Leaders in 2008.[16] They are the only set of common standards adopted and used by more than forty-three states. The purpose was to create policy standards to help state policy makers strengthen selection, preparation, licensure, and professional development to ultimately provide leaders with the tools they need to be successful and create consistency among leaders. The six standards organize the functions that define strong school leadership and represent the high-priority areas educational leaders need to address to promote the success of all students. They call for:

1. Setting a widely shared vision for student learning;
2. Developing a school culture and instructional program conducive to student learning and staff professional growth;
3. Ensuring effective management of the organization, operation, and resources for a safe, efficient, and effective learning environment;
4. Collaborating with faculty and community members, responding to diverse community interests and needs, and mobilizing community resources;
5. Acting with integrity, fairness, and in an ethical manner; and
6. Understanding, responding to, and influencing the political, social, legal, and cultural contexts.

The previous lists attempt to discern what should be common practice for school leaders and frame the lessons described in the following chapters. There is one additional specification of skills that bears attention in this review. The sample of principals we have studied have all achieved success in relatively high-poverty and/or high-minority schools. Martin Haberman, from the University of Wisconsin, using data from multiple studies of effective principals and working from the NPBEA platform for practice, identified thirteen dimensions of successful school leadership for principals in high-poverty settings (see table 2.2).[17] He argues that schools serving poor children are often in large, ineffective bureaucracies that create innumerable barriers to success which are more challenging and disruptive than what other principals experience. However, within

Table 2.2: Haberman's dimensions of effective urban school leadership

Sensitive to diversity vs. insensitive to diversity	Predicts the principal's ability to be perceived as fair and equitable in an urban school serving diverse children, parents and community in poverty.
Sets a common vision vs. fosters personal preferences	Predicts the likelihood that the principal will create the effective work teams and cooperative activities needed for the school to succeed, rather than seek to make individuals happy by following their preferences.
Develops positive working climate vs. enforces rules	Predicts the principal's potential for creating a positive working climate, as opposed to having the school function as a depersonalized bureaucracy.
Instructional leader vs. building manager	Predicts whether the principal will function as the school's leading educator, rather than the overseer of the school organization and the physical facility.
Data-driven vs. idiosyncratic	Predicts the ability of the principal to increase the effectiveness of the school in achievement, attendance, suspensions and in other critical areas where the data is readily available.
Product evaluation vs. process evaluation	Predicts whether the principal will maintain a focus on improved learning as the ultimate value to be preserved, or whether the programs in his/her school will be evaluated on the basis of procedures followed and how the programs are implemented.
Personal accountability vs. others' accountability	Predicts the respondent's willingness to hold him/herself accountable for people and processes which s/he cannot completely control.
Responsible leader vs. delegator	Predicts the degree to which the principal perceives him/herself as directly and personally responsible for major school functions.
Expanded principal's role vs. traditional role	Predicts the principal's propensity to connect the school with the resources needed to serve diverse children in urban poverty, or to be limited to only the district's budget, personnel, and resources.

Table 2.2: Haberman's dimensions of effective urban school leadership (cont.)

Client advocate vs. staff advocate	Predicts the principal's ability to serve diverse students and families in poverty while simultaneously representing the professional staff.
Bottom-up representative vs. top-down representative	Predicts whether the principal will protect and enhance effective practices in his/her school or simply follow orders.
Parents with a voice vs. parents as helpers	Predicts the likelihood that the principal will seek to involve parents and community as genuine partners, or limit them to homework helpers and visitors.
Problem solver vs. reactor	Predicts whether the principal will be a dynamic, creative leader, or whether s/he will passively wait for problems and solutions to be presented to him/her.

Source: http://www.habermanfoundation.org/StarAdministratorQuestionnaire.aspx.

these systems, he was able to identify highly effective principals and wanted to learn more about their practice given that they succeeded in spite of the conditions around them, when others did not. The principals helped identify "best practices" that they felt led to their success.

The thirteen dimensions represent administrators' behaviors and predispositions to act, which differ from the other specifications of effective school leadership. Each dimension is defined as a dichotomy (e.g., Creates a Common Vision / Fosters Personal Preferences). Principals are rated high, acceptable, or low on each dimension based on the results of an assessment. These actions reflect an ideology regarding the respondents' beliefs about the nature of effective schooling for diverse children and youth in urban poverty and the nature of school leadership necessary to create such schools. The questionnaire Haberman developed was completed by a majority of the principals in our research to see how they would rate on these standards and to complement the qualitative data collected. The data from the questionnaire will be shared in chapter 3.

WHAT DO PRINCIPALS DO DAY TO DAY?

Other types of research have been ongoing to better understand the job of principal. These focus less on orientations, beliefs, and skills and instead focus on actions, tasks, and behaviors that can be observed. Before this body of literature, surprisingly little was documented about what principals do every day. This additional research tried to remedy that and, as well, examine if any variability in behaviors existed across principals in different schools that might be related to effectiveness. Methodologies have included ethnography, self-report, and more recently diaries and experience sampling, where principals respond to intermittent pages and record their actions, who they were with, and where they were.[18] The latest research in this line of questioning had researchers shadowing principals and recording their activities every five minutes to eliminate self-report bias and to allow for more detailed descriptions of their time use.[19]

The research finds that principals engage in over forty different kinds of tasks daily, reflecting the real complexity of the position and challenges inherent in staying focused, something the It's Being Done principals are tenacious about, as we will see in later chapters. These tasks are typically grouped into larger categories that reflect the major responsibilities of a principal that were discussed in the last section, including administrative/managerial, instructional, and cultural. Generally, the findings reveal that principals are more likely to be engaged in administrative and managerial activities as opposed to instruction-related activities including classroom observations and professional development for teachers. For example, one study found principals' activities were primarily administrative (63.4%) followed by curriculum and instruction–related tasks (22.5%), fostering relationships (8.7%), and professional growth (5.8%).[20] Managing students (20.5%), one of the tasks classified as administrative, was done nearly as frequently as attending to the more than twelve tasks associated with curriculum and instruction. The distribution of time reflects the draw toward the managerial or maintenance role of the job, even as the field calls for "instructional leadership," and a principal's intention may be otherwise.[21]

Another study used similar categories but further differentiated the administrative and instructional categories to better understand what aspects of leadership were related to school performance since principal time on day-to-day instructional activities was so small and only marginally, if at all, related to student outcomes.

The principals could have been involved in any one of six main activity types: administration (27%), organization management (21%), day-to-day instruction (6%), instructional program (7%), internal relations (15%) or external relations (5%), or another activity that did not fit, which accounted for almost 19 percent of the recorded actions (e.g., having lunch or transitioning). The distribution of time was consistent with other research findings, that principals' activities are more likely to be managerial (administrative and management ~50%), with instructional leadership accounting for less than 15 percent of their total time. Also, principals spent most of their time in their own offices (54%), with another 9 percent in the main office and only about 8 percent of the school day spent in classrooms. Principals at all school levels, and within high/low poverty or high/low minority settings, spent their days similarly and generally seemed to be caught up in the administrative responsibilities of the job. However, the study found that greater time spent on organizational management activities was associated with positive school outcomes measured by test score gains as well as teacher and parent assessments of educational climate. The authors concluded that effective instructional leadership must combine an understanding of the instructional needs of the school with an ability to target resources where they are needed, hire the best available teachers, provide teachers with the opportunities they need to improve, and keep the school running smoothly. This point will be elaborated in later chapters by the qualitative data we collected from principals that describes their actions in relation to improving instruction in their schools. The It's Being Done principals call themselves instructional leaders and do prioritize time in classrooms and providing feedback to teachers, but they also think strategically about how to leverage their managerial responsibilities to support the achievement goals they have identified.

One final study bears mentioning. Its goal was not to document all tasks the principal engaged in but rather to simplify the list and understand what, of all the possible roles and tasks a principal may do, they actually do and what other responsibilities are taken up by other staff members.[22] In particular, the study asked the question, Do all principals need to possess all the skills defined generally in the ISLLC standards? Instead of observing behavior day to day, principals, teachers, and department heads were interviewed to understand how their schools distributed leadership and management responsibilities and identified and solved problems. The schools included in the study were of a broad range in terms of quality and achievement for students, unlike this study, which focused on exemplars and also high-poverty and high-minority settings. Also, they studied different types of schools (N=21) in an effort to identify constants in school leadership from challenges that are particular to certain types of schools (e.g., being part of a district).

The study had three interrelated findings that reflect much of the prior research, but it makes a different point and sets up some of the research questions that we asked of leaders who had clearly led school improvement or successful schools. Specifically, the authors concluded that school leaders have to be master diagnosticians. How they diagnose, interpret, and analyze situations and determine solutions is the key measure of their success. This study suggests that leadership depends on context, and a principal needs to understand the particular needs, talents, and resources of their school. This is not unlike what we found with the It's Being Done principals, who will be analyzed in greater detail within the chapters ahead.

HOW AND HOW MUCH DOES LEADERSHIP AFFECT STUDENT LEARNING?

First, it must be said, for a long time following the publication of the Coleman Report, many educators believed schools really did not have much of an impact on student learning.[23] Each student was thought to have a personal glass ceiling on educational attainment due to their heredity, family background, and socioeconomic status. The effective schools movement, which developed in opposition to this notion that schools were unimportant, started to change this thinking. Research began to document that some schools were more effective than others; the search for what inputs, variables, and processes made a difference was underway. The body of research from this movement convincingly refers to the need for strong leadership from the principal.[24] Edmonds singled out the principal as the most significant person in the creation of an effective school and went so far as to say that without a strong administrator, "elements of strong schooling cannot be brought together or kept together."[25] Similarly, Dow and Oakley state, "The research on school effectiveness has identified a number of factors that appear important in identifying effective schools. One factor that appears consistent in all of the studies is principal leadership."[26]

The effective schools movement proved to be a catalyst for research, beginning in the 1980s, about the role of the principal and what behaviors of the principal affect student outcomes most. Research has alternately tried to describe how the principal exerts an effect, explicitly trying to quantify just how large the effect is and, further, what behaviors contribute most to that effect.

The effective schools case studies suggested a large effect by the principal, but there was little statistical evidence that this was so, and Eric Hanushek and others were pointing to teacher quality as the primary reason for the observed difference in student and school outcomes.[27] Eberts and Stone were the first to attempt to test the conclusions drawn from the case studies of principal effectiveness with actual student achievement and not just the process of learning.[28] Using a national sample of elementary schools (N=14,000), they created measures of principal behavior and attributes and examined their relationship with student outcomes. They also explored the various paths through which effective principal behavior was transmitted to students. They found principal leadership in instructional activities (e.g., setting priorities and evaluating instructional programs) and in conflict resolution (establishing consensus on objectives and methods, maintaining effective discipline) were important to student achievement, but leadership outside these areas was not. These findings were confirmed with a national sample of high schools, which began to lend evidence to the belief about the importance of principals and just how they could go about impacting achievement in their schools.[29]

With this emerging quantitative support, multiple studies of the effect of principals were conducted, most of which confirmed the original conclusions of the effective schools movement; however, there were discordant voices, and the size of the effect varied from small to large. As a result, a number of thorough reviews of the literature were conducted to better understand and quantify the effects of principals on student outcomes.[30] For example, Hallinger and Heck synthesized forty-three studies conducted between 1980 and 1995.[31] They found that there were three types of studies about principals: direct effects of leadership practices; indirect effects whereby the principal influence was mediated by other people or organizational factors; and interactive effects between leadership efforts and environmental factors that went back and forth. The general pattern of results reconfirmed that principals matter, but also found their influence was primarily indirect and, as such, small. Although the overall effect was reported to be relatively small, it was statistically significant and interpreted as a meaningful school variable.

Across the studies, generally leadership is thought to explain 5–7 percent of the variation in student learning *across* schools, which may sound small, but accounts for about a quarter of the total across-school variation explained by all school-level variables, after taking into consideration student background characteristics.[32] The within-school effects are likely large, given the case study reports and additional quantitative data from teachers and parents, which suggests that the quality of the principal affects teacher satisfaction, a teacher's decision about where to work, and parents' perceptions about the school.[33] The paths through which leadership influences student learning are by and large considered to be school goals, school structure, teachers, and organizational culture.

Marzano, Waters, and McNulty take the research one step beyond just estimating the size of the total leadership effect, which they describe as a correlation of about .25, and try to separate what is essential from merely important in an effort to help practitioners make use of the research.[34] They identify twenty-one specific leadership responsibilities and estimate each dimension's average effect size to help principals know where to direct their effort (see table 2.3). Interestingly, the relationship between each of the leadership responsibilities and student achievement is within

Table 2.3: Twenty-one responsibilities and their correlations with student academic achievement

Responsibility	The extent to which the principal:	Effect size
Affirmation	Recognizes and celebrates accomplishments and acknowledges failures	0.19
Change agent	Is willing to challenge and actively challenges the status quo	0.25
Communication	Establishes strong lines of communication with and among teachers and students	0.23
Contingent rewards	Recognizes and rewards individual accomplishments	0.24
Culture	Fosters shared beliefs and a sense of community and cooperation	0.25
Discipline	Protects teachers from issues and influences that would detract from their teaching time or focus	0.27
Flexibility	Adapts his or her leadership behavior to the needs of the current situation and is comfortable with dissent	0.28
Focus	Establishes clear goals and keeps those goals in the forefront of the school's attention	0.24
Ideals/beliefs	Communicates and operates from strong ideals and beliefs about schooling	0.22
Input	Involves teachers in the design and implementation of important decisions and policies	0.25
Intellectual stimulation	Ensures faculty and staff are aware of the most current theories and practices and makes the discussion of these a regular aspect of the school's culture	0.24

Table 2.3: Twenty-one responsibilities and their correlations with student academic achievement (cont.)

Responsibility	The extent to which the principal:	Effect size
Involvement in curriculum, instruction, and assessment	Is directly involved in the design and implementation of curriculum, instruction, and assessment practices	0.20
Knowledge of curriculum, instruction, and assessment	Is knowledgeable about current curriculum, instruction, and assessment practices	0.25
Monitoring/ evaluating	Monitors the effectiveness of school practices and their impact on student learning	0.27
Optimizer	Inspires and leads new and challenging innovations	0.20
Order	Establishes a set of standard operating procedures and routines	0.25
Outreach	Is an advocate and spokesperson for the school to all stakeholders	0.27
Relationships	Demonstrates an awareness of the personal aspects of teachers and staff	0.18
Resources	Provides teachers with materials and professional development necessary for the successful execution of their jobs	0.25
Situational awareness	Is aware of the details and undercurrents in the running of the school and uses this information to address current and potential problems	0.33
Visibility	Has quality contact and interactions with teachers and students	0.20

Source: Robert Marzano, Timothy Waters, and Brian McNulty, *School Leadership That Works: From Research to Results* (Alexandria, VA: Association for Supervision and Curriculum Development, 2005), 42–43.

a narrow range. The responsibility with the strongest relationship was Situational Awareness—or a principal's attention to and reaction based on the particular details of the school. This reaffirms the need for principals to be master diagnosticians, an aspect of It's Being Done principals explored in subsequent chapters.

WHAT IS THE ROLE OF THE PRINCIPAL IN HIGH-POVERTY SCHOOLS?

An emerging interest has been to analyze high-poverty, culturally diverse schools, given the transition to standards-based reform and accountability. Is the principal's role in these schools different?

The Chicago Consortium on School Research (CCSR) has been studying school reform in Chicago since the 1990s, when the city began implementing a decentralization plan to help improve schools.[35] They found that local control facilitated improvement in a number of schools and that the principal was largely responsible for whether a school moved forward or not. Three common elements of successful principals were identified. First, the leadership style of effective principals was characterized by a focus on student learning, effective management, and a reliance on both pressure and support to motivate staff. Second, the practices they employed were strategic. Principals started by dealing with problems that could be solved quickly, but created a long-term improvement agenda to create coherence. Third, they focused on key issues, including building ties with the community; developing teacher knowledge and skills; and promoting a school-based professional community. These practices are similar to how the principals' role is generally characterized. But this research also suggests an idea seen elsewhere in the literature and widely held in the profession—that there are unique problems and barriers that the principal of a high-poverty urban school must address. And there is also a different type of urgency about the work.

As this work in Chicago moved forward and it was clear that some schools were improving and others were not, CCSR initiated an intensive longitudinal study of the internal workings and external conditions that distinguish improving from stagnating schools, which resulted in a model of school improvement.[36] Among the five essential supports for school improvement, school leadership was identified as the driver for change, corroborating the findings of the effective schools research from the 1970s with a current population of schools facing very different expectations and accountability.

Another case study of high-poverty schools added a further dimension to this work that resonates with our findings and seems to be essential to leading well in schools that need to dramatically improve. "Simply put," the authors concluded, "our cases clearly demonstrate that this job is not for the faint of heart. It takes courage, persistence, as well as leadership knowledge and skills, to be successful in high-poverty challenging schools."[37] Principals in high-poverty schools face additional barriers as the schools and communities are often resource-poor, and research has shown that poverty can interfere with a school's ability to achieve success with all its students. But these principals are not deterred by the barriers poverty can produce and do not use these conditions as excuses for poor performance. And, as will be seen with the It's Being Done principals in later chapters, education is viewed as the vehicle for changing the conditions, so they never blame students for poor performance and instead focus on what they can do so their students have the same opportunities as other more privileged students.

A recent study conducted in elementary "Honor Schools of Excellence" (N=24) in North Carolina, some with large gaps (>15%) and some with small gaps (<15%) in achievement between white and minority students, identified specific differences in practices between the leaders that may reflect how they operationalize these beliefs.[38] After establishing that small-gap schools do not differ significantly from large-gap schools in terms of observable teacher quality measures or student populations, the researchers examined qualitative data to establish an explanation for some of the small gap–large gap variation. The authors find three major differences between principals of small gap and large gap schools: (1) Principals of small-gap schools deliberately celebrate student achievement using overt strategies (quarterly rewards, notes home, positive report cards, etc.); (2) Principals of small-gap schools offered feedback and support to teachers in an effort to improve teaching and learning; and (3) Principals in small-gap schools expect all students to learn, whereas principals in large-gap schools doubt the notion that all students can learn.

Similarly, but at the high school level, the Achievement Gap Initiative at Harvard University recently held a conference featuring 15 public high schools.[39] Most of the schools had achieved unusually high value-added test score gains in at least one subject and narrowed test-score gaps between all of their racial/ethnic groups and whites in the rest of the state. The conference report distills specific strategies that schools designed and implemented to achieve and sustain their improvement. The central theme is that skilled principals developed leadership teams that focused relentlessly on monitoring and supporting high quality teaching and learning. The most effective schools created detailed rubrics for judging the quality of student work; the most effective principals required all teachers to participate in professional development focused on helping students meet the standards of those rubrics. In several cases, transformations produced far better outcomes for students than many teachers thought were possible.

Finally, one additional study deserve mention as it attempts to document barriers and actual practices of leaders to work through issues that arise in high-needs settings.[40] Theoharis analyzed six principals who were committed to social justice and had evidence of success with populations of traditionally marginalized students. The study finds that justice-minded principals have to combat four patterns of injustice in schools: school structures that marginalize students (such as pull-out special education services); a staff that lacks confidence or skills to reach every child; a disconnect between the school and the community; and low student achievement. The six principals combated each using the following strategies:

- Eliminated pull-out/segregated programs
- Increased rigor and access to opportunities by, for example, creating heterogeneous classes
- Increased student learning time by, for example, increasing attendance rates or minimizing transition time
- Increased accountability systems measuring student achievement
- Addressed issues of race with the staff
- Provided ongoing support around equitable practices

- Hired new teachers with justice-oriented mind-sets
- Empowered staff through relationship building
- Created a warm environment for students
- Reached out to marginalized families in the community
- Incorporated social responsibility into academic content areas.

This body of work on principals in high-poverty schools sets the stage for our work. This work suggests the role is the same or at least the responsibilities are, but that there are additional challenges and barriers about which the principal needs to take immediate and strategic action. We are specifically interested in extracting broad lessons about leadership in high-poverty schools and describe our methodology below.

STUDY OF IT'S BEING DONE PRINCIPALS: SAMPLE, METHODOLOGY, AND DATA COLLECTED

This idea of equity and excellence is critical to our work. We wish to understand leadership in this context, as this is what the It's Being Done principals have achieved (see their descriptions in chapter 1 and why they are worthy of study). We set out to understand how successful principals, as the leaders of their schools, improve educational practices and student learning for all students. What characteristics, behaviors, goals, and practices are shared among the principals? What differences exist and why? How do they prioritize competing demands of the job? The research has established core responsibilities and practices for principals, and we discuss our results in relation to those broad areas of responsibility, including setting a vision, establishing the instructional program, managing the building, creating the culture and climate within the school, and managing relationships outside the school with the district and community. Ultimately, we hope to understand the job of the principal in relatively high-poverty schools in greater depth and to tell the stories of these exemplary leaders who accomplished both equity and excellence in their schools.

The research reported here is the third part of an ongoing project of The Education Trust to identify and learn from highly effective schools for low-income and minority students. Two previous books, authored by Karin Chenoweth, *It's Being Done* and *How It's Being Done*, established that high-poverty and high-minority schools could help students excel and documented the practices of educators within the building. Over the course of conducting this work, it became obvious that the leaders of these schools were the critical link and their practice was worthy of study on its own. They do not attribute the success of the schools to themselves, but as outside observers we can see what a pivotal role the leaders and their leadership played. Unlike the prior two books, which told the individual stories of schools, a district, and a state, this book attempts to combine the principals into a group and find themes that are shared. To help decipher if these shared ideas are integral to their success, we use existing data from a national survey of principals to have a sample to compare them to, and we also "test" them out on a survey that is used to select principals who are likely to be successful in high-poverty, urban settings.

Our final sample of principals (N=33) come from twenty-four schools across the country (see table 2.4). The schools, at all levels (62% elementary), differ in size and are located in different locales and parts of the country. Most are regular, neighborhood public schools; one is a charter school. The average free and reduced-price lunch across the schools is 75 percent, and the average minority student enrollment is 73 percent.

Our primary methodology is a case-study approach. This method has two primary benefits, the first being that we learn from the wisdom of those who have actually done work in their own words: What do they believe is important and why? There are not many examples of successfully improving schools; case studies provide a method to capture this knowledge. Case studies also allow for in-depth learning; our questions focus on collecting practical, detailed information. Research often doesn't have obvious implications for practitioners, but we hope to describe specific strategies and practices that others can adapt and apply. There are also limitations to case-study research. Case studies are retrospective, so it can be hard for individuals to remember and map step-by-step how they went from poor performance to improvement, to sustained growth and success. Case studies also have limited generalizability; it is impossible to say with certainty what caused the outcomes and that the same strategies will work in all types of schools.

Table 2.4: School characteristics

Characteristic	Frequency	Mean (SD)
Level		
Elementary	62.5%	
Middle	12.5%	
High	12.5%	
Combined	12.5%	
Locale		
Urban	54.2%	
Suburban	20.8%	
Rural	25.0%	
School size		
<200 students	0.0%	
200–499 students	50.0%	
500–799 students	25.0%	
>799 students	25.0%	
Percent of students receiving free or reduced-price lunch (FRL)		
<25%	4.2%	
25%–50%	12.5%	
50%–75%	25.0%	
>75%	58.3%	
Percent of students who are minorities		
<25%	4.2%	
25%–50%	16.7%	

Table 2.4: School characteristics (cont.)

Characteristic	Frequency	Mean (SD)
50%–75%	25.0%	
>75%	54.2%	
Mean school size		667.1 (452.2)
Mean percent FRL		74.8% (23.4)
Mean percent minority		73.0% (23.1)
N=24 schools		

Source: Common Core of Data, 2009–2010, http://nces.ed.gov/ccd.

Visits and observations have been conducted at all the schools over the past few years of the project. While at the schools, staff and students were interviewed, and classrooms and meetings (e.g., data meetings or professional learning communities) were observed. We understand that these visits only represent a slice of time, but additional phone calls and e-mails have clarified inconsistencies and been used to gather additional insights. In addition, state reports and artifacts from school Web sites have been collected and analyzed.

In addition to this data, we collected new information, with the principal as the primary informant. We include principals who led improvement as well as principals who sustained high performance. In addition, a few assistant principals responded to the three surveys, as they were, for all intents and purposes, functioning as coprincipals during the tenure of the primary principal. Our intention was to collect the same information or have the principals respond to the same questions to ensure consistency so that we could learn what commonalities existed and where they diverged. Our three data collection tools are described in the following section; the full sets of questions are included in appendixes A and B at the end of this chapter.

Schools and Staffing Survey (SASS): Principal Questionnaire. This survey is administered to a nationally representative sample of principals every three years by the U.S. Department of Education. From the full sample, we also selected a representative sample of principals in high-poverty schools (>70%), whose official federal status was Needs Improvement. These principals are likely teaching in similar types of schools as the principals we are studying, so we use them for comparison as well. Topics covered in the survey include educational background, experience, primary goals, perceived influence, and teacher evaluation.

The Star Urban Administrator Questionnaire. This survey was developed and is administered by the Haberman Educational Foundation at the University of Wisconsin–Milwaukee. School districts across the country administer it to aspiring principals to see if they would be a good match for the position. It is a proprietary survey, so the questions are not included in the appendix, but in broad terms, it attempts to collect information about the dispositions and behaviors of principals through 104 forced-choice questions. The thirteen dimensions assessed on the survey were previously described in this chapter (see table 2.3).

Education Trust Principal Interview. The survey includes fifteen open-ended questions designed to probe the principals' practices in a deeper, more qualitative way in order to understand why what they did increased student achievement. Topics covered include their perception of the role of principal, their initial goals, factors that contributed to success, and the decision-making process at their school.

Our analysis proceeded in multiple steps. First, a set of descriptive data was compiled for each of the schools from the National Center for Education Statistics, Common Core of Data, and school report card data. Second, the quantitative data from the Schools and Staffing Survey was added to the school descriptions. The data were examined in relation to school type to see if any clear differences emerged that may be relevant to the case studies. Third, we received the results from the Star Urban Administrator survey (N=21). We analyzed the results to learn how the principals scored on each of the dimensions and also to see if any differences emerged by school type. Finally, we coded and summarized the individual interviews in multiple ways and reviewed the artifacts collected about each school. We prepared case studies of the individual schools. We used an inductive, grounded theory approach to look for indicators of categories and themes within responses to individual questions, across principals and schools, which we named, coded, and summarized quantitatively. The basic idea of the grounded theory approach is to read (and reread) the data collected, in this case interviews with school leaders, and to "discover" categories, concepts, and properties and their interrelationships.

CONCLUSION

The school principalship is not a black box. In fact, it has received intensive scrutiny, and a growing body of evidence has demonstrated the effect of principal leadership on student learning and the extra importance of leadership in low performing schools. Indeed, according to The Wallace Foundation's Learning from Leadership Project: How Leadership Influences Student Achievement, "The total (direct and indirect) effects of leadership on student learning account for about a quarter of the total school effect."[41] Furthermore, another study funded by the Wallace Foundation concluded, "To date, we have not found a single case of a school improving its student achievement record in the absence of talented leadership."[42]

Equity and excellence is a newer idea, demanded by standards-based reform and accountability policies, and one that is not embraced by those who believe that poverty and its effects are too great to overcome. Poverty can exert a powerful influence on learning, but we believe schools can and must do better for children living in poverty, and the schools and principals profiled here are leading the way.

APPENDIX A

The Education Trust Principal Survey, Part 1

(Adapted from the School and Staffing Survey, 2007–08)

1. Enter your name and school below.

2. How many years did you serve as principal of the above school or any other school? (Skip if you are an assistant principal.)

3. Before becoming the principal of the above school, how many years did you serve as the principal of a school? (Count part of a year as 1 year.)

4. Before you became a principal, how many years of assistant principal experience did you have? (For assistant principals, count all years of experience as assistant principal.)

5. Before you became a principal or assistant principal, how many years of elementary or secondary teaching experience did you have?

6. What is the highest degree you have earned?
   - Do not have a degree
   - Associate degree
   - Bachelor's degree (B.A., B.S., etc.)
   - Master's degree (M.A., M.A.T., M.B.A., M.Ed., M.S., etc.)
   - Educational specialist or professional diploma (at least one year beyond master's level)
   - Doctorate or first professional degree (Ph.D., Ed.D., M.D., L.L.B., D.D.S.)

7. If you have a master's degree or higher, is it in Education Administration?
   - Yes
   - No
   - If no, what type of degree is it?_____

8. We are interested in the importance you place on various educational goals. From the following nine goals, which do you consider the most important, the second most important, and the third most important? (Only choose three of the nine goals below.)

	Most important	Second most important	Third most important
Building basic literacy skills (reading, math, writing, speaking)	☐ 1	☐ 2	☐ 3
Encouraging academic excellence	☐ 1	☐ 2	☐ 3
Promoting occupational or vocational skills	☐ 1	☐ 2	☐ 3
Promoting good work habits and self-discipline	☐ 1	☐ 2	☐ 3
Promoting personal growth (self-esteem, self-knowledge, etc.)	☐ 1	☐ 2	☐ 3
Promoting human relations skills	☐ 1	☐ 2	☐ 3
Promoting specific moral values	☐ 1	☐ 2	☐ 3
Promoting multicultural awareness or understanding	☐ 1	☐ 2	☐ 3
Fostering religious or spiritual development	☐ 1	☐ 2	☐ 3

9. How much actual influence do you think you have on decisions concerning the following activities?

	No influence	Minor influence	Moderate influence	Major influence
Setting performance standards for students of this school	☐ 1	☐ 2	☐ 3	☐ 4
Establishing curriculum at this school	☐ 1	☐ 2	☐ 3	☐ 4
Determining the content of in-service professional development programs for teachers of this school	☐ 1	☐ 2	☐ 3	☐ 4
Evaluating teachers of this school	☐ 1	☐ 2	☐ 3	☐ 4
Hiring new full-time teachers of this school	☐ 1	☐ 2	☐ 3	☐ 4
Setting discipline policy at this school	☐ 1	☐ 2	☐ 3	☐ 4
Deciding how your school budget will be spent	☐ 1	☐ 2	☐ 3	☐ 4

10. How often is professional development for teachers at this school:

	Never	Rarely	Sometimes	Frequently	Always
Designed or chosen to support the school's improvement goals?	☐ 1	☐ 2	☐ 3	☐ 4	☐ 5
Designed or chosen to support the district's improvement goals?	☐ 1	☐ 2	☐ 3	☐ 4	☐ 5
Designed or chosen to support the implementation of state or local standards?	☐ 1	☐ 2	☐ 3	☐ 4	☐ 5
Evaluated for evidence of improvement in student achievement?	☐ 1	☐ 2	☐ 3	☐ 4	☐ 5
Considered part of teachers' regular work?	☐ 1	☐ 2	☐ 3	☐ 4	☐ 5
Planned by teachers in this school or district?	☐ 1	☐ 2	☐ 3	☐ 4	☐ 5
Presented by teachers in this school or district?	☐ 1	☐ 2	☐ 3	☐ 4	☐ 5
Accompanied by the resources that teachers need (e.g. time and materials) to make changes in the classroom?	☐ 1	☐ 2	☐ 3	☐ 4	☐ 5

11. What percentage of students had at least one parent or guardian participating in the following events?

	0-25%	26-50%	51-75%	76-100%	Not applicable
Open house or back-to-school night	☐ 1	☐ 2	☐ 3	☐ 4	☐ 5
All regularly scheduled schoolwide parent-teacher conferences	☐ 1	☐ 2	☐ 3	☐ 4	☐ 5
One or more special subject-area events (e.g. science fair, concerts)	☐ 1	☐ 2	☐ 3	☐ 4	☐ 5
Volunteer in the school on a regular basis	☐ 1	☐ 2	☐ 3	☐ 4	☐ 5

12. Please choose one grade at your school. Answer the following two questions for the grade you have chosen. If your school does not have a third or eighth grade, skip the following two questions.
    - 3
    - 8

13. How long is the typical full week of school for students? (Please report in minutes, e.g., 30 hours and 0 minutes = 1,800 minutes, 32 hours and 54 minutes = 1,974 minutes, etc.)

14. During a typical full week of school, approximately how many minutes do most students spend in the following activities at this school?

    (If most students have courses taught on a rotational schedule, calculate typical course time based on the following example: For a course taught 60 minutes a week for half the year, respond with 30 minutes per week. Do not include time spent on additional tutoring or remedial instruction for students receiving special services. Total should not exceed the number of minutes answered in number 13. If your school does not offer a particular activity for students during the typical week, put a 0 in the box.)
    - English, reading, or language arts
    - Arithmetic or mathematics
    - Social studies or history
    - Science
    - Foreign language (not English as a Second Language)
    - Physical education
    - Music
    - Art
    - Recess

15. What percentage of your time do you spend on each of the following responsibilities during a typical school day? (Your answers should sum to 100%.)

    Administrative Tasks: Responsibilities include managing schedules, managing student discipline, managing student attendance, preparing/implementing standardized tests, and fulfilling compliance requirements.

Organizational Management: Responsibilities include managing budget, hiring personnel, dealing with concerns from staff, and maintaining campus facilities.

Day-to-Day Instructional Tasks: Responsibilities include formally and informally evaluating teachers, implementing professional development, teaching students, and using data to inform instruction.

Instructional Program Tasks: Responsibilities include developing an educational program, evaluating the curriculum, using assessment results for program evaluation, planning professional development, and utilizing school meetings.

Internal Relations Tasks: Responsibilities include developing relationships with students, teachers, and parents and attending school activities.

External Relations Tasks: Responsibilities include working with local community members, fundraising, and communicating with the district to obtain resources.

    _____ Administrative Tasks
    _____ Organizational Management
    _____ Day-to-Day Instructional Tasks
    _____ Instructional Program
    _____ Internal Relations Tasks
    _____ External Relations Tasks

16. How many full-time K–12 classroom teachers in your school would you put in the following categories, based on your overall opinion of their teaching abilities?

Outstanding Teachers: These teachers' levels of skills, knowledge, and professionalism are exceptional. You would easily nominate them for teaching awards due to their performance in the classroom. They make excellent examples to other teaching faculty members.

Good Teachers: These teachers' levels of skills, knowledge, and professionalism make them successful teachers in the classroom. You are glad to have them as part of your faculty, but they are not at the very top of teachers for their grade and subject.

Fair Teachers: These teachers only exert the effort necessary to get the job done in the classroom. They do an adequate job but are not exemplars for other teachers. They could potentially improve with proper on-the-job training or coaching.

Unsatisfactory Teachers: These teachers have levels of skills, knowledge, and professionalism that are inadequate, and at present they do not belong in the teaching profession.

    ___ Outstanding Teachers

    ___ Good Teachers

    ___ Fair Teachers

    ___ Unsatisfactory Teachers

17. Including hours spent during the school day, before and after school, and on the weekends, how many hours do you spend on all school-related activities during a typical week at this school?

18. How many total hours do you spend interacting with students during a typical full week in this school?

19. Are you male or female?
    - Male
    - Female

20. Are you of Hispanic or Latino origin?
    - Yes
    - No

21. What is your race? (Mark one or more races to indicate what you consider yourself to be.)
    - White
    - Black or African American
    - Asian
    - Native Hawaiian or Other Pacific Islander
    - American Indian or Alaska Native

Note: This appendix was reproduced from a survey by The Education Trust. Used with permission.

APPENDIX B

The Education Trust Principal Survey, Part 3

1. How did you come to occupy the principalship?
   - Applied
   - Drafted

2. If you were drafted, how did you initially react?

3. Were you confident that you could do the job? Why?

4. Briefly, how do you define your role as principal?

5. Briefly, how do you define a successful student?

6. What is your school's mission and how do you communicate this to key stakeholders?

7. What was the context of the school when you took over (e.g., culture, teaching, district/community support, etc.)?

8. What was your initial goal when you took over the principalship and what steps did you take to meet it? How did your goals change over time?

9. What are the two or three most important factors that contributed to your school's success/improvement? What was your role, as leader, in bringing about those things?

10. What is the decision-making process in your school about key issues (e.g., schedule, budget, hiring, etc.)?

11. When you are faced with competing, legitimate priorities between or among staff, students, or parents, what guides your decision and how do you explain it to staff?

12. What do you do when a new initiative from the central office could contradict, complicate, or replace a program/structure in your school that is producing good results?

13. What is the greatest challenge that you have faced during your tenure as principal of this school? How did you handle the situation?

14. Low-income and minority children are often not expected to achieve at high levels. How did you address beliefs about student learning and communicate about expectations to students, teachers, and to the community?

15. If you could ask legislators for two or three things that would substantially help you in your job, what would you ask for? What about from your district?

16. What resources have you drawn upon to learn your job and to maintain your enthusiasm?

17. Is there something more that you would like to add to help us understand your role as a school leader?

Note: This appendix was reproduced from a survey by The Education Trust. Used with permission.

CHAPTER THREE

At the Starting Gate

What It's Being Done
Principals Bring to the Job

In chapter 1, we laid out the evidence for what makes this particular set of thirty-three principals worthy of study. Looking across the sample, it would be hard to identify any one common external characteristic of the leaders. They are both relatively young and longtime veterans. They are male, female, black, white, Asian, and Latino. They went to private colleges and public universities. They come from middle-class backgrounds and low-income families. They do all work long hours. Being a principal of a high-needs school is not an easy job. It requires a significant commitment of time, which is true of any executive job. Principals are responsible for managing staff, budgets, and a physical space. Moreover, school leadership is an enterprise about growing and preparing students for active citizenship through curriculum and instruction. This learning is done in the context of relationships, which are not turned off when the school bell rings. Principals make phone calls to families and community service providers and attend events after school and on the weekends. It is not a 9–5 job, and the hours add up. The data show, though, that the It's Being Done principals do not work significantly more hours than other principals of high-needs schools or other principals in general (see figure 3.1).

In addition to working hard, some clear themes emerge regarding their preparation for the job of principal and the way they think about educating children that are particularly relevant to leading success in high-poverty and high-minority schools. This chapter describes their prior education, experiences and core beliefs about student success as well as how they rated on the Star Administrator survey and how they compare against a national sample of principals.

BECOMING THE PRINCIPAL

To be a principal requires administrative certification or licensure, at least for all traditional public schools. Charter and private schools are not always bound by the same rules, but in general, certification is necessary, and to earn that certification, an advanced degree is required. So, all the It's Being Done principals had the necessary licensure to assume the job. But only about half of them sought out the principalship of their It's Being Done school. A number of the leaders were comfortable as classroom teachers and had to be pried out of the classroom. This is not uncommon in the field; quite a few teachers earn administrative certification for the additional pay without becoming administrators.[1] John Capozzi, principal of Elmont High School, once joked about the principalship, "Who would want the job; it's horrible!" For educators who love teaching, the job of principal is often associated with meetings, headaches, and less time with students. But many of these principals were recruited by individuals who saw their potential as school leaders and who nudged them into the position. Both Arelis Diaz and June Eressy were surprised when they were approached. Neither had considered administration, and Eressy even went further to say, "Oh, no—not me—I belong in the classroom. I felt that I had very big shoes to fill and that I was just 'getting good' in the classroom—I felt that school leadership was not my niche."

In our sample are both "original" principals—principals who led initial changes in the school—and "sustainers," most of whom worked with the original principal and came in to sustain the improvement. Both originals and sustainers were relatively evenly split on whether they applied or were drafted for the position. The sustainers who applied for the position had worked in the school for years and believed they were the right person for the job. They had experience teaching the students, knew the culture of the building, needs of the community, and in many cases had been included in priority decision making during the tenure of the

Figure 3.1: Number of hours principals report working

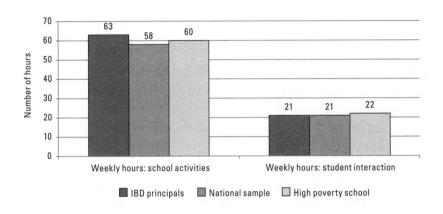

Source: Schools and Staffing Survey, 2007–2008, The Education Trust Principal Survey, Part 1, questions 17 and 18.

prior principal through both formal and informal leadership teams that had been established. They understood how the school operated to meet the students' needs and felt compelled to carry on what had already been established. This is a different type of responsibility and pressure than that of the "original" principals who led the initial improvement. Where sustainer principals felt a responsibility to ensure the school remained a success, original principals felt compelled to make an immediate difference for the students who were languishing in struggling schools.

One of the sustainer principals drafted for the job was the P.S./M.S. 124 assistant principal, Valarie Lewis. She relates that she was molded, while working under Elain Thomson's direction, without realizing what she was being molded into. "I got pulled along with the tide of change. It becomes a vehicle that you want to keep driving." Lewis was aware of the pull of outside demands on a principal working in a school in New York City. She knew what she would like to be able to do, and was "crazy enough to get the job done," but following an external district blueprint was rather daunting to consider. In this context, Lewis said that flexibility was essential to her being a successful principal. The other principals did not use this word specifically, but it was clear that they relied on this trait to handle the myriad of situations they were confronted with during their tenure.

READINESS FOR THE PRINCIPALSHIP

Whether they applied for the principalship or were drafted, most of the principals reported feeling confident that they could do the job. Every principal talked about at least one of two key factors that helped them feel confident and capable of leading a school: their prior instructional experience, or mentorship and training by another principal.

Their confidence, by the way, did not necessarily mean they also weren't anxious about the awesome responsibility being undertaken, particularly when first being confronted with extremely low student performance. As Natalie Elder said, "At first I didn't know *not* to be confident. Then I saw the test scores. I knew of the school; I just didn't know it was in such bad shape!"

Almost all our leaders spent time as teachers, and their teaching experience proved a source of confidence for many different reasons. First, it helped the principals know what students ought to know and be able to do—the content of schooling—but it also shaped their beliefs about how much students could learn. They knew that some students have disadvantages which make learning harder, but their experiences had showed them that students can go further than what might be expected and that teachers can, with disciplined inquiry into practice, push past those expectations. Molly Bensinger-Lacy put it this way: "I had learned from my students that they were capable of learning just about anything of which I was capable of teaching them." And Susan Brooks adamantly stated, "I wouldn't accept failure in my students as a teacher; I needed to find a way to reach and teach them and I did."

Second, because they knew instruction, the It's Being Done principals were confident they could help other teachers be better teachers. They think of themselves as teachers and, as they often expressed, principals are just teachers of teachers. This is a role they know, rely on, and feel comfortable with; they define their jobs as creating learning experiences for adults to help them reach their potential. Ricci Hall sums this up quite elegantly: "Being a school leader is complicated. More than being about budgets or bottom lines, more than being about evaluations or meeting attendance, being a school leader is about helping to create powerful learning experiences for your staff and faculty and creating the circumstances where teachers can do the same for their kids."

Finally, their experience in the trenches afforded these principals credibility with their new school staffs that eased the transition. Teachers and school people generally are not quick to trust people who have not walked in their shoes, and their years of teaching meant that teachers could not dismiss them as ignorant of the realities of classroom teaching and instruction.

On average, the principals in this study had almost eleven years of classroom teaching experience before becoming principal. This is actually very similar to the national average of most principals at 12.7 years.[2] A small minority of the principals had five or fewer years of classroom experience, but more than ten of the It's Being Done leaders had fifteen or more years of classroom teaching experience.

The one notable exception was Von Sheppard, principal of Dayton's Bluff Achievement Plus Elementary School in St Paul, Minnesota, known as one of the worst-performing schools in the state in 2001 when he took over. Sheppard had had no classroom teaching experience but was a college football player and coach and had worked as an assistant principal. His large and imposing frame immediately established his authority in the school, but his coaching experience was even more valuable. He immediately set to work establishing academic achievement goals for the students and creating plans to measure progress.

The teaching experience of the It's Being Done leaders was not entirely as traditional classroom teachers. A number were special education teachers or teachers of English language learners. This type of teaching, more so than traditional classroom teaching, requires the instructor to think individually about each child, be persistent, and try new strategies in an effort to promote learning and reach each child. Jennie Black, assistant principal at Ware Elementary School, said that her eight years of teaching special education had prepared her well for the assistant principal's job as it had required a "significant amount of leadership, data analysis, management and mentoring of paraprofessionals," all of which she felt were essential in being an effective leader.

In addition to their teaching experience, It's Being Done principals cited the role of mentors and formal and informal apprenticeships as important for their confidence and efficacy.

Dolores Cisneros-Emerson's experience was a combination of planned and unplanned training opportunities. She had been an administrator at another school before arriving to lead Morningside Elementary School. She describes her previous school as high achieving with a low rate of poverty. While at that school, her principal had provided her with many opportunities to make decisions and learn additional skills. One year she put together the school's budget; in other years she filled in as school secretary and data-entry clerk when those positions were vacant, allowing her to do what she called "walking in the shoes" of other school employees. She was also fortunate to learn what not to do as well. Her principal pointed out her own mistakes in an attempt to prevent Cisneros-Emerson from having to learn the same lessons the hard way. Through those experiences, Cisneros-Emerson felt prepared to take on the principalship of high-poverty Morningside Elementary School.

Conrad Lopes, the original principal of Jack Britt High School, had a similar experience. He worked as an assistant principal for five years, under what he describes as "really good principals" who allowed him to learn all aspects of the job from scheduling to budgeting. When he became principal of Jack Britt he felt it was his responsibility to do the same for his assistant principals and provided mentorship and structured experiences for them, which paid off. One of his former assistant principals, Denise Garison, is now principal and has sustained the school's success. She, in turn, is mentoring her assistant principals to take on greater responsibilities so that they, too, might have the opportunity to become principals.

William Austin, at Roxbury Prep Charter School, in Boston, was selected by existing school leaders to take on the coprincipal position. The school was a well-functioning school when he took over; it was, however, in the midst of a facilities and student-body expansion, which required leadership to maintain the high student performance they had achieved as a smaller school. In addition to knowing he had the support of mentors who selected him for the position, he was also in a unique position, feeling that the staff would work hard to ensure his and the school's success.

ON-THE-JOB EXPERIENCE

Although most It's Being Done leaders had extensive classroom teaching experience, most did not have extensive assistant principal or principal experience prior to becoming principal. On average, the group had only about two or three years of actual administrative experience as either an assistant principal or principal before becoming principal of the It's Being Done school for which they are recognized. A majority of the leaders had no principal experience before taking over the It's Being Done School; three had more than ten years of principal experience, while the remaining had generally fewer than five years of experience. More than a quarter of the original principals had no assistant principal or principal experience (see figure 3.2).

EDUCATION

As mentioned earlier, advanced degrees are an entry requirement for the job of principal so, of course, the It's Being Done principals have master's degrees. But almost half also have an advanced certificate beyond their master's degree, and another 15 percent have earned a doctorate. A sizable majority of principals earned their degree in educational administration, which is the typical program of study for a leadership position, but a few had training in some specific content, including gifted education, urban education, applied linguistics, special education, or counseling and guidance.

This data, along with comments the principals made during the qualitative interview and reading lists provided to us, tell us that they have a thirst for knowledge and are interested in knowing what is going on in the field whether through traditional course work, attending conferences, reading professional journals, or the hot education books circulating in the field. They then take this knowledge, see if it matches their core beliefs, inte-

Figure 3.2: Prior experience among It's Being Done principals and comparison groups

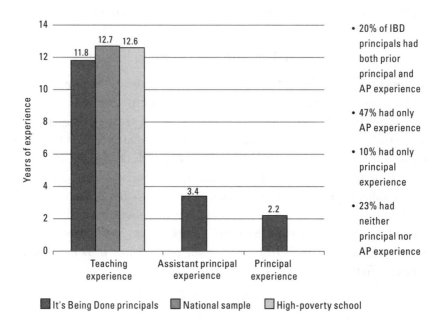

- 20% of IBD principals had both prior principal and AP experience
- 47% had only AP experience
- 10% had only principal experience
- 23% had neither principal nor AP experience

■ It's Being Done principals   ■ National sample   ☐ High-poverty school

Source: Schools and Staffing Survey, 2007–2008, The Education Trust Principal Survey, Part 1, questions 3, 4, and 5.

grate it into what they know, and further develop their toolbox of skills. Molly Bensinger-Lacy described having a knack for applying knowledge to practice, but this knack is really based on hard work and a desire and interest to improve. School and book knowledge is part of the equation, but what they are doing is striving to be on top of their game. They also actively try to surround themselves with staff who also want to learn and, as Denise Garison said, "I am not afraid to ask questions."

Tom Graham said, "We laugh at ourselves and try to learn." And they may just like being students as much as they like being teachers.

"I have had the pleasure of earning a Ph.D. in Special Education and going on to take an additional 55 hours of coursework in school administration and educational psychology," said Cynthia Kuhlman. "I love being a student as well as a teacher and school leader."

Figure 3.3: How do It's Being Done principals define a successful student?

Source: The Education Trust Principal Survey, Part 3, question 5, and www.wordle.net.

VISIONS FOR STUDENT SUCCESS

One of the key responsibilities of a leader is to help members of a school achieve unity of purpose. The principal's vision of student success, which always includes academic mastery, provides that purpose, and the It's Being Done principals make it their job to translate those general ideas into courses of action.

But It's Being Done principals do not define the success of their students narrowly (see figure 3.3). To them, successful students are defined by curiosity, confidence, and a sense of joy in learning. At the elementary level, the principals are more likely to talk about successful students learning to be good citizens; at the secondary level, principals are more likely to talk about successful students being ready to succeed in college and careers. The point is that all have ambitions for their students that are much broader than simply passing state tests and meeting grade-level expectations. For example, Elain Thompson explained, "Unfortunately, success for many people is just data. Success for me is to see a child grow physically, emotionally, intellectually, and socially. If I have a child who comes from a shelter, if they can acclimate and can go to their teachers with trust and say, 'I didn't have breakfast this morning'—that confidence will help them become a better student. I had kids score off the charts, but these were sometimes the same kids who were smuggling liquor into the building."

Keep in mind that these principals were identified because of the very high test scores of their students. And yet they do not define a successful student as one who does well on tests but, rather, more broadly as someone who applies himself, loves to learn, and is able to stand up for himself.

"You know what a successful student is?" said Mary Haynes-Smith of Bethune Elementary. "A successful student is one who achieves as much as he is capable of achieving. One who can articulate his feelings, who is not afraid to ask questions, who will challenge you, who will stand up for himself in a positive way. You don't have to make all A's, but if you can walk around and feel successful, that's a successful student. One who is learning what he is capable of learning—and we know they are all capable of learning."

So, when forced to rank the goals they have for students, how do principals respond? Their answers to such a question from the Schools and Staffing Survey distinguish them from other principals of high-needs schools (see figure 3.4). Generally, all principals are more likely to choose five of the nine goals, including academic mastery, basic skills, work habits, personal growth, and social skills. There is one notable difference in the rankings, however. It's Being Done principals are much more likely than the national sample—particularly the sample of principals of high-needs schools—to say that "academic excellence" is their top goal for students. Other principals are more likely to say "basic skills," something It's Being Done principals rate below academic excellence. This seemingly slight distinction seems to make a lot of difference in practice.

These findings take on additional significance when we consider the huge debate around federal accountability provisions that have been in place since 2001, requiring schools to make continual academic progress as measured by state reading, math, and science tests. Critics claim—and some research suggests—that "test-based accountability" has led to schools narrowing their goals to simply pass state tests, which in turn

Figure 3.4: It's Being Done principals place the highest value on excellence followed by basic skill acquisition and work habits

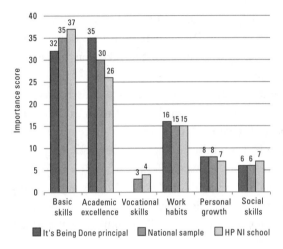

What do you consider to be the three most important educational goals?

- Building basic literacy skills (reading, math, writing, speaking)
- Encouraging academic excellence
- Promoting occupational or vocational skills
- Promoting good work habits and self-discipline
- Promoting personal growth (self-esteem, self-knowledge, etc.)
- Promoting human relations skills
- Promoting specific moral values
- Promoting multicultural awareness or understanding
- Fostering religious or spiritual values

Source: Schools and Staffing Survey, 2007–2008, The Education Trust Principal Survey, Part 1, question 8.

forces schools to focus their instruction very narrowly on basic reading and math skills, driving out curiosity and creativity.[3]

That isn't how this set of highly successful principals thinks or acts. They want their schools to provide rigorous instruction and actively engage students in the learning process. They want their students—many of whom are poor or racially isolated—to gain access to the opportunities their more privileged peers have, with all that implies for enjoyment of travel, culture, and access to the power and responsibilities incumbent upon those of us who live in a democracy. It's Being Done principals understand that for their students to gain access to those opportunities, they *should* have an education that is defined quite broadly, but they *must* at least have mastered the knowledge and skills required by colleges, high-skill technical programs, and the military.[4]

That means that they prepare students for state reading and math tests, which may not be excellent measures of a good education but do provide some indicators of whether students are prepared for the future and, moreover, provide practice for the tests that will face students at entry points throughout their lives.

"I make no apologies for helping prepare my students to take tests," said Molly Bensinger-Lacy of Graham Road Elementary School. "I hope when the SAT comes around, they will know how to take it as well as any middle-class student whose parents paid for SAT prep classes."

So they help their students understand how tests are constructed and what kinds of skills and knowledge different kinds of tests ask students to demonstrate. That is part of what explains their good state test results.

But the important thing to remember is that It's Being Done principals say over and over again: this is just a small part of what we do. "We don't teach the tests, we teach the standards," is what many say. Visiting these schools confirms that tenfold. Teachers are engaging students in rich curriculum opportunities, and not providing endless drill-and-kill instruction.

CORE BELIEFS ABOUT EDUCATION

All It's Being Done leaders believe deeply that every one of their students can be successful if the learning environment is the right one. And they believe it is up to them as principals to create that learning environment.

They see education as the path out of poverty and isolation and believe deeply that it is the job of schools to teach all kids—even the most impoverished and isolated—to high levels. The following four quotes are examples of just how strongly they believe this work can be done and that it is, in fact, their job to make sure it happens.

"There are no learning gaps in children, only opportunity gaps," said Deb Gustafson, principal of Ware Elementary. "It is our job to close the opportunity gaps."

"It's the learning environment that determines the success and motivation of the student to achieve," said Susan Brooks, former principal of Lockhart Junior High School.

"All students are successful given the right instruction," said Barbara Adderley, former principal at M. Hall Stanton Elementary School.

Figure 3.5: Results from Star Administrator Survey, It's Being Done Principals

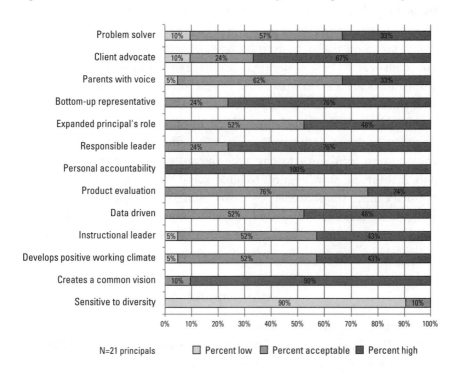

N=21 principals   ☐ Percent low ☐ Percent acceptable ■ Percent high

Source: The Star Urban Administrator Questionnaire, Haberman Educational Foundation at the University of Wisconsin–Milwaukee, http://www.habermanfoundation.org/StarAdministratorQuestionnaire.aspx.

"I believe that a solid education is sometimes the only chance in life for low-income students," said Melinda Young, former principal of Wells Elementary School.

The results from the Haberman Star Administrator survey strongly support and confirm this belief with quantitative data (see figure 3.5). As discussed in chapter 2, Haberman identified thirteen dimensions of effective practice for urban principals teaching children in poverty. Almost all of the twenty-one principals who took the survey scored acceptable or high on all of the dimensions identified by the survey as important for principal selection. Meeting the established criteria reflects a belief about the necessity of rigorous schooling for diverse children and youth in poverty and the responsibility of school leadership to create such schools by making difficult choices. In addition, most or all of the principals scored high on five of the dimensions. Those areas were personal accountability, common vision, responsible leader, bottom-up representative, and client advocate. These dimensions emphasize the responsibility of principals to advocate and do what is in the best interests of students, above all else, and to ensure their staff shares that vision.

Almost all the principals scored low in one dimension: sensitivity to diversity. We can't definitively explain this finding, but we suspect that the question format might partly be the answer, rather than the principals' inability or unwillingness to understand the importance of race and ethnicity. Since they have largely closed achievement gaps and have high-functioning schools for all students, it appears they are not limited by negative perceptions of race and ethnicity that color their choices and judgments.

CONCLUSION

There exists no shortage of ideas about what good school leadership entails. In chapter 2 we saw that myriad lists and frameworks define the core knowledge, skills, and abilities thought to be essential for principals. Pop culture also presents a vision of how principals of urban schools should act and what they should know and be able to do. Joe Clark, as portrayed in the film *Lean on Me*, was often seen walking around Eastside High School with a bat and locking students in the building, suggesting that being a principal simply requires toughness.

The experiences and beliefs of It's Being Done leaders speak to something else entirely. Deeply embedded in the craft of instruction, their experience in classrooms helps them understand the potential of children and the power educators have to help them learn.

CHAPTER FOUR

First Things First

Being an Instructional Leader

Not long ago, principals were simply expected to be administrators.

No one should think that "simply" implies that administering a school well is in any way simple or easy. It means managing the building, which includes budgets, schedules, staff, students, food service, transportation, and parent communication; it also means handling discipline, preventing and managing crises, and, at the secondary school level, running a sports and extracurricular program. There's plenty on that list to keep anyone busy without ever touching the instructional core of a school. It is no wonder that a highly lauded retired principal recently said, "It never once occurred to me that it was my job to increase student achievement."

But the days of simply administering a school are gone; today, principals are expected to lead academic improvement in their schools.

Even if that's the new reality, it is taking a while for the field to catch up. Just recently we heard about a teacher who was attracted to a principal-preparation program by the idea that he could affect the education of more children than is possible for a single teacher. Experienced principals mentoring him, however, told him that 80 percent of the job is pure administration; he found that discouraging enough to wonder whether he made the right decision to pursue administrative credentials. Putting the best face on it, the old hands are trying to help their young colleague from having his hopes dashed by alerting him to the way the job has worked for them. But they also exemplify how old realities clash with new expectations.

It's Being Done principals provide a striking counterexample, both in how they think about the job and what they do with it.

It's Being Done leaders define themselves primarily as instructional leaders (see figure 4.1). The management responsibilities of a principal never go away, but these high performing principals see their core job as ensuring that each and every student is learning a great deal, which means they spend the bulk of their time and energy on making sure students have rich, coherent instruction with deep intellectual challenges, a school atmosphere conducive to teaching and learning, and excellent teachers. They work hard not to allow their administrative responsibilities to distract them from those central tasks. In fact, as we will discuss in chapter 5, they go further, working to ensure that the management functions they are responsible for support their instructional role. As Gary Brittingham, the former principal of East Millsboro Elementary, said: "I was the instructional leader first, closely followed by school manager. The two are so closely related that it is hard to separate."

To understand why It's Being Done principals are so adamant about their instructional role, it is helpful to remember that they see education as a path out of poverty and isolation and believe deeply that it is the job of schools to teach all kids—even the most impoverished and isolated—to high levels.

As we saw in chapter 3, It's Being Done leaders believe deeply that all their students can be successful if the learning environment is the right one. And they believe it is up to them as principals to create that learning environment.

> 100% of It's Being Done principals scored high along the personal accountability dimension on the Star Administrator Survey.
>
> The personal accountability dimension measures the likelihood that the principal will hold him/herself accountable for student learning, even when many factors are out of his/her control.

In defining their role this way, they have taken on a huge responsibility. It is hard enough to run a school where some children learn. To ensure that all students learn at high levels requires that countless moving parts

Figure 4.1: Definition of role

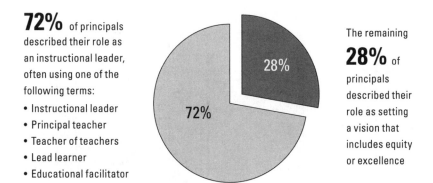

72% of principals described their role as an instructional leader, often using one of the following terms:
- Instructional leader
- Principal teacher
- Teacher of teachers
- Lead learner
- Educational facilitator

The remaining **28%** of principals described their role as setting a vision that includes equity or excellence

Source: The Education Trust Principal Survey, Part 3, question 4.

work together seamlessly, and It's Being Done principals hold themselves responsible for making sure all the parts work together. That does not mean they do everything. Much the way pilots take responsibility for everything that happens on their planes without actually maintaining the engines and fueling the tanks, It's Being Done leaders don't make every decision and fulfill every role. What It's Being Done leaders do is harness the efforts of everyone in their buildings to work toward the same goals. As Diane Scricca, former principal of Elmont Memorial High School said, "It's not my job to run the building. It's everybody's job."

They do this by exerting the power that many principals don't recognize they have over having a clear vision of student and school success; setting uncompromising standards of performance; putting in place the policies, procedures, and systems to ensure that all adults in the building understand the vision and are able to make incremental, measurable improvements toward the goal; and continually monitoring results (see figure 4.2).

SETTING A VISION—AND A SYSTEM TO MONITOR IT

It's Being Done leaders begin by having a clear vision for the mission of their schools.

Figure 4.2: Principals' perception of influence over organizational structures to support learning

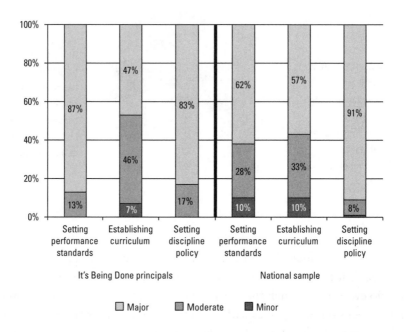

It's Being Done principals   National sample

□ Major   ▨ Moderate   ■ Minor

Source: Schools and Staffing Survey, 2007–2008, The Education Trust Principal Survey, Part 1, question 9.

Most schools in the country have mission statements, and many of them are elegant expressions of aspiration about building lifelong learners and helping all students learn to their maximum potential. It's Being Done schools are no different in this regard, and their leaders take their missions seriously. "The purpose of a mission statement and a vision is to move the school," said Barbara Adderley, former principal of Stanton Elementary. Along the same lines, John Capozzi, principal of Elmont Memorial High School, said: "We teach it, we display it everywhere, we model it, and we live it every day."

But most schools have an underlying ethos that lies beneath their formal mission statements, which is where the true nature of the school can be seen. For It's Being Done schools, this could be summed up by Lockhart Junior High School's motto, plastered at the school entrance: "100 Percent

Success, Every Child, Every Time." Or, as Dolores Cisneros Emerson, principal of Morningside Elementary, said: "The [stated] mission is to ensure we challenge every child to do their best. The real school mission is not to let any student fail."

Part of the way It's Being Done leaders make their school missions real is by setting very concrete standards of performance for students. So, for example, Gary Brittingham of East Millsboro Elementary School said, "All schools have lofty statements. Our real mission was that all students would meet the state standards for academics and that at least 60 percent would achieve above the minimum passing standards."

> 100% of It's Being Done leaders believe that all their students not only can learn but can meet and exceed state standards.

All It's Being Done leaders have the goal that all their students will meet or exceed state standards. That doesn't mean that minimum proficiency is all they expect. As we discussed in chapter 3, It's Being Done leaders are much more ambitious than that for their students. But by expecting all students to meet and exceed state standards, they are expressing in a concrete way the mission that all students will be successful.

School leaders do not set that expectation without acknowledging the obstacles. "Sometimes we look at the children coming in and wonder how we're going to get them to meet standards," said Molly Bensinger-Lacy of Graham Road Elementary School. "They come in so behind."

But Bensinger-Lacy, like her fellow It's Being Done principals, knew that if she didn't hold firm that all students must achieve, it would be all too easy to slip into complacency.

After all, many of the children in It's Being Done schools arrive at school so behind their peers that helping them be less behind would be considered a major accomplishment in many schools. When students make progress, it can be easy for teachers to lose sight of how far away they still are from meaningful performance standards. Good teachers want to congratulate and encourage their students, and understandably shy away from saying, "You made real progress but you're still two grade levels below where you should be." It's Being Done leaders want that teacher to go on to say, "I know you will get there and I am going to make sure that you do."

This is why Bensinger-Lacy, when teachers presented her with evidence of a student's progress, would celebrate the progress and then say something like, "Yes, he certainly has grown, and if he doesn't move faster he is likely never to graduate from high school or go to college."

This is an uncomfortable role, but it is one that It's Being Done leaders take on. They understand that they are the guardians of their students' academic futures and must be the one who names what Bensinger-Lacy calls the "elephant in the room."

By setting the uncompromising standard that all students must not just make progress toward standards but meet or exceed them, It's Being Done principals create tangible goals that can be clear to everyone in the building—students, parents, teachers, and staff.

But It's Being Done Leaders don't just express the goal of student success. They put into place systems to ensure that every teacher understands that the goal of success applies to each student and require a plan for every student in the school.

So, for example, when Cynthia Kuhlman was principal of Centennial Place Elementary, she sat down with every teacher every semester with all the classroom records to discuss each student—how the student was doing and what the teacher had planned to ensure that the student met standards; if the student had already met or exceeded standards, the teacher needed to have a plan to provide enrichment and extension. Together they also looked at patterns of achievement—perhaps all the children in a particular class had mastered two-digit multiplication, for example, so Kuhlman would make sure that teacher would demonstrate to colleagues what she was doing. At the same time, however, 80 percent of the teacher's students might not have understood the rules of capitalization, so perhaps the teacher needed to learn from her more successful colleagues or go to a workshop or conference that would help her teach that topic.

At Bethune Elementary, Mary Haynes-Smith has a slightly different process—she and her instructional leaders, including the reading and math coaches, sit down with each teacher and her records once a month to review individual student data and look at patterns of achievement, alert to any signs that teachers might need additional information or help in teaching a particular topic or subject. They are adamant that good instruction is the best motivator for students. But because they serve poor, isolated children in New Orleans—a city that still struggles to emerge from rubble—they watch for any sign that students are losing enthusiasm and succumbing to despair. When they notice one, they think together of what more could motivate and energize them—perhaps a volunteer mentor or a field trip to expand their horizons and make them appreciate the world that is open to educated people.

Barbara Adderley and Molly Bensinger-Lacy, in larger elementary schools, would meet with grade-level teams once a week to go over student achievement data and have the same kinds of conversations about what to do if students hadn't met standards and what to do if they had.

In secondary schools, much of this work of going over individual teacher data is done by department chairs and assistant principals, with the principal monitoring the work of the other administrators. But even at Elmont Memorial High School and Jack Britt High School, each of which have almost two thousand students with more than one hundred teachers, principals John Capozzi and Denise Garison keep a close eye on the data of any teacher with higher than average numbers of failures and make sure they have plans in place to improve their instruction.

By regularly monitoring the progress of individual students and the plans teachers have to improve performance, It's Being Done principals combine the establishment of performance standards with support for teachers in a continual process where one feeds into the other and builds a sense not only that children can meet standards but that teachers are capable of helping them do so. As Sharon Brittingham said, it was not enough for teachers to believe that all students could learn. "Teachers have to believe that they can teach all children."

By establishing routines to monitor how individual students are doing in relation to standards, It's Being Done leaders are challenging a deep-rooted sense that schools and teachers can't have much effect on student achievement, particularly for students who live in impoverished neighborhoods with few resources. To those outside the education field, this might seem odd. After all, why even have schools if not to affect student achievement?

But the conventional wisdom among academics in teacher preparation programs and elsewhere, dating from 1966 with the publication of the Coleman Report,[1] has been that the social capital children bring with them to school trumps any effect that schools can have. Children from poor backgrounds and, sometimes, from minority groups, are often judged to be so hopelessly behind that schools can be expected to provide only a very limited education. Poverty in particular has been documented to present challenges that are considered insurmountable for all but a few lucky children.

The constant drumbeat that schools can have little effect has left many teachers in high-poverty and high-minority schools with the belief that trying to teach all their students is futile and will only lead to burnout and despair. Coupled with the fact that they often teach in schools that are not organized for them to be successful, this has resulted in many eager and committed teachers reaching what one former superintendent calls "a disappointed place in their own heart." It has taken an almost heroic ability for great teachers to persist in providing great instruction to all their students in the typical high-poverty and high-minority school dominated by discouragement.

CONFRONTING ATTITUDES ABOUT WHO CAN ACHIEVE

To those teachers who have become discouraged, or who never had high expectations for all children, It's Being Done principals have found that they often need to address head-on the expectations that teachers have for poor children and children of color.

"I use myself as an example," said Mary Haynes-Smith of Bethune Elementary in New Orleans, referring to the fact that she grew up poor in New Orleans, like many of her students. "It's a fallacy that poor children can't achieve. We do that all year long, through staff meetings and our vision. We just keep telling people that all people can learn."

Some are even more uncompromising. "Every single child can learn and achieve. If you don't believe it, you shouldn't be in education," said Carmen Macchia of Port Chester Middle School in Westchester County, New York.

"I just don't buy into low expectations," said Morningside Elementary's Dolores Cisneros-Emerson, along the same lines. Teachers who do, she said, "are welcome to apply for a job on the other side of town."

This idea that it is the job of educators to believe in the ability of every child is very powerful among this group of principals, and comes up again and again. "I didn't care where these kids came from," said Von Sheppard, of Dayton's Bluff Achievement Plus Elementary School in St. Paul, Minnesota. "[I] didn't care whether or not they had family support (which many did not), didn't care if they were low-achieving, special ed, ELL, or mentally impaired . . . our job was to teach them!"

Many It's Being Done principals came to this understanding from their own experience as classroom teachers, where they worked to ensure success for all their students. Valarie Lewis, for example, began working at P.S. 124 in Queens in a cramped basement room with too many children, including many with disabilities who at the end of the year were able to "graduate" from having a special education classification. "Don't tell me what children can't do," she says. Similarly, Arelis Diaz and Molly Bensinger-Lacy both spent years teaching children of recent immigrants and saw the strides that students arriving at school with little or no English could make with good instruction.

In fact, one of the reasons Bensinger-Lacy took the job at Graham Road Elementary, she said, was that "I had learned from my students that they were capable of learning just about anything of which I was capable of teaching them." When she arrived at Graham Road she found a staff, she said, that asked very little of their students; failure seemed inevitable because they knew that their students brought in so little in the way of academic wherewithal. In her first meeting with teachers, Bensinger-Lacy shared some of the research on effective schools, such as the work of Ron Edmonds from the 1970s and 1980s.[2] She also referred to the 90/90/90 schools identified by Doug Reeves, as well as information about a local school with similar demographics that was doing better than Graham Road.[3] "I continued to pass on such information as it became available," she said.

But she didn't leave it at that. "Whenever anyone in the school would start 'blaming the victim,' I would say, without fail, something like, 'Yes, it is true that this child has this particular challenge. Now what are we going to do to level the playing field for him so that he can become a better reader?'" With that, Bensinger-Lacy acknowledged reality—which is that many poor children arrive ill-prepared for school, with relatively small vocabularies, limited background knowledge, and family lives that don't always support academic achievement—but made sure the conversation was about what the school could do to make them successful despite those facts.

All It's Being Done principals have versions of that story as examples of how they help teachers raise their expectations, but they often keep their focus on changing actions rather than beliefs. "Changing beliefs has to be done through showing people, not telling people," said Sharon Brittingham, former principal of Frankford Elementary School in Delaware, who told her teachers that even if they didn't believe all children could learn, they were paid to act as though they can and said that they must teach all children to the same level. At the same time, she got the teachers additional help and training in teaching reading, writing, and math. When student achievement improved, she used the results as an example of the difference changes in instruction can make.

Similarly, Barbara Adderley addressed the issue of low expectations among teachers at Stanton by "establishing professional learning communities and daily grade-group meetings and doing book studies and changing how we implemented instruction in the classrooms and [holding] meetings to talk about how to support failing children."

In other words, Adderley built a new kind of professional culture with systems and procedures that supported teachers, which in turn built a sense of efficacy among the teachers that they could get all their students to succeed.

ALL MEANS ALL—WHICH MEANS INDIVIDUALIZING

Here we need to acknowledge that even It's Being Done principals make an exception to the word "all" in the case of children with profound cognitive impairments. While It's Being Done leaders certainly expect their students with severe cognitive impairments to learn and progress, most agree that some children may never meet state standards.

But that small exception, which usually works out to no more than 1 percent of children, does not mean that It's Being Done principals grant a blanket exception for all children with learning disabilities. When It's Being Done principals sit down with their teachers to go over the data for individual students, they do not want to hear, "He's special ed" as a reason for why the student is not achieving. They want to hear what scaffolding, what pre-teaching, and what re-teaching the teachers are doing to ensure that the student with a learning disability is learning enough to meet standards. If the teacher is unsure or needs additional help, It's Being Done leaders help think through how an aide or paraprofessional might work with an individual student or a small group of students who are struggling with the same topic; how the teacher might be freed from other responsibilities to work one-on-one with a struggling student; or how an instructional coach or special educator might be helpful in thinking about different ways to teach.

Many It's Being Done principals have found that focusing on the needs of individual students and getting them help as soon as an issue arises has reduced the percentages of students who need to be formally identified as having learning disabilities. They also find that this attention to the needs of individual students handles many of the common issues that students with learning disabilities often have.

For example, when Gary Brittingham was still principal at East Mills-boro Elementary, he said that he was very surprised at some of the 504 plans some children would bring with them from their previous schools. A 504 plan is an artifact of federal law which requires that schools spell out how they will accommodate the disabilities of children. Different from Individualized Education Programs, which are required for students whose disabilities qualify them for special education services, 504 plans often specify, for example, that teachers must write down all homework assignments for students with auditory processing disabilities, or provide seating at the front of the class for students with Attention Deficit Disorder.

"You shouldn't need a federal law for that," Brittingham said. "That's just good instruction."

This is the way that It's Being Done principals think about instruction—that it is the job of professional educators to structure learning so that each individual child will be successful. When students are unsuccessful, they believe it reflects on the instruction.

George Hall's Terri Tomlinson summed up the attitude of all It's Being Done principals when she said, "We understand why a student might not do well on a test. But if all the students don't do well, that's got to reflect back on the teacher. We don't ever blame the students in this building—in fact, we try not to place any blame. What we do is look for solutions."

Diane Scricca, former principal of Elmont Memorial Junior-Senior High School, put a slightly different twist on this: "When teachers don't feel that they can do it and they don't have support, they start blaming kids and they say, 'Oh, these kids, I can't work with them, they don't do their homework, their parents don't help, what do you expect me to do?' That's a teacher who doesn't have the pedagogical set of skills to make a difference in their classroom. That's the sign of a school that has become dysfunctional—when you start pointing at what the kids didn't do rather than what you can do to make it better."

It's Being Done leaders understand that it is their job to help ensure teachers are prepared to "make a difference in their classrooms," and they do that in large part by what many of them call "empowering" teachers.

CREATING A SYSTEM TO EMPOWER TEACHERS

A few years ago there was a movement to do what some called "teacher-proofing" instruction. Teacher-proofing was an attempt to reduce the variability that is inherent in the traditional way instruction has been organized. Traditionally, each teacher has decided just about everything about instruction, from topics, assignments, and pace to grading for their classroom. That level of teacher autonomy has led to the fact that in most schools, students—particularly those students whose families don't have the wherewithal to notice problems and intervene—are entirely dependent on their individual teachers for what they learn in a given year. A good fourth-grade teacher means you learn long division. A bad one means you don't.

"Teacher-proofing" attempted to reduce the variability that students experienced by ensuring that all students would have at least a certain level of quality instruction. Teachers—often in high-poverty and high-minority schools, where variability has been demonstrated to have devastating effects—were required to "deliver" scripts within a tightly bound curriculum.

It's Being Done principals have taken a different tack. They also work to provide a floor by making sure students have a common curriculum, assignments, and assessments. But instead of teacher-proofing, which many teachers find demoralizing, they do it in a way many call "empowering." That is, they work to ensure that teachers in their buildings are knowledgeable, skillful professionals who understand what children need to know and be able to do and who can use a variety of teaching techniques to teach them.

Naturally, this means they pay close attention to hiring teachers, a topic we will address below.

But It's Being Done leaders also understand that no matter how good, no one teacher can be expert enough in every content area and pedagogical technique to be able to help all students succeed.

"DE-PRIVATIZING" TEACHING

One of the essential paradoxes of instruction is that good teaching is highly dependent on expert teachers, yet no teacher can be expert enough to teach all things to all children. It's Being Done leaders solve this by doing what Richard Elmore of Harvard University has called the "de-privatization" of teaching.[4]

De-privatizing means that teachers tackle instructional issues together, pooling their knowledge and expertise in a systematic way so that all children succeed.

At its most basic, de-privatizing means that teachers at the same grade level or who teach the same class are working on the same things more or less at the same time with the same assessments and the same performance standards. When they do so they are able to observe each other, learn from each other, and help each other in a deep way.

So, for example, teachers who are teaching quadratic equations at the same time are able to have deep conversations about what problems they are giving their students, how they are explaining them, and how their students are doing. When one teacher's students don't do well on a quiz, she is able to go to colleagues who are teaching the same material and ask them to observe or make suggestions about what they have done. If none of them is successful teaching a topic, they can together research what outside materials exist or what workshop or conference might be helpful.

Good teachers have always built these kinds of collaborative relationships when they have been lucky enough to have cooperative colleagues. But It's Being Done school leaders do not leave this to the vagaries of personal interest and desire. They make this the core of the way their schools work.

In their schools, teachers work together to unpack standards, map out a scope and sequence of lessons, develop assessments and assignments, study data together, and work together to improve their content knowledge and teaching techniques by observing each other teach, sharing ideas, and learning new things. At the elementary level this work is mostly done in grade-level teams and occasionally across grade-level teams; at the high school level within departments; and, in middle school grades, both. At all times, the focus is on what It's Being Done leaders consider the key questions:

- What do the students need to know?
- How do we teach it?
- How do we know if they've learned it?
- What do we do if they didn't learn it and need extra instruction?
- What do we do if they did learn it and need extension and enrichment?

This book will not examine in detail the work done within those teams. Some of it is described in *How It's Being Done: Urgent Lessons in Unexpected Schools,* but educators who want to really understand how to unpack a standard, map curriculum, build assessments, and use data to propel improvements in instruction will have to read other books. In this book we are focusing on the role of It's Being Done leaders in building this kind of collaborative culture. As leaders they are making choices and compromises that often fly in the face of conventional wisdom and tradition and as such can be unpopular with staff members—at least initially. This is understandable because they are putting into place a completely different way of operating. Teachers long used to what they call "autonomy," where they are in control of everything that happens within their classrooms, often find becoming part of a system focused on student achievement disconcerting. They are being asked, in essence, to become part of a team where once they were lone operators. This same issue is being faced in medicine where doctors are asked to be less "cowboy" and more "pit crew" in order to produce better outcomes for patients.[5]

Because professional literature has emphasized the need to de-privatize teaching for the past decade, many school administrators now understand that teachers need the opportunity to collaborate with colleagues and schedule times for collaboration. But that doesn't mean that they know how to help teachers benefit from those structures. One teacher at North Godwin Elementary talks about her previous school where the school's daily collaboration often devolved into "gripe sessions about the kids and the parents."

The leaders in our study understand that most teachers are unfamiliar with systems of collaborating that will help students, and know it is incumbent on them to help teachers learn new ways of working. As a result, they structure the work carefully by setting agendas for collaborative meetings, and either they or another administrator participates to ensure that the meeting doesn't get sidetracked by other conversations. They are adamant, for example, that meetings not be dominated by the usual fare—field trip reports, announcements of new roll call systems, and all kinds of what could be called "administrivia" that can usually be conveyed by email. Most educators have stories of meetings where memos are read to them. That is exactly the kind of thing that It's Being Done leaders work against.

"Time is our most precious commodity, and we must use it effectively and wisely," said Deb Gustafson, principal of Ware Elementary. "In terms of school improvement, school leaders must not waste teacher or student time. Therefore, meetings and requirements must be well organized, focused, agenda-driven, and contain specific expectations."

With a principal who sets clear expectations for collaboration, the North Godwin teacher mentioned above who had such a bad experience with collaboration in her old school is now part of a cohort of new teachers who meet regularly to discuss research articles and consult each other and senior educators about instruction; she is also a key member of a grade-level collaboration team that has a packed agenda for every meeting with no time for griping—even if the members had the inclination. Sometimes the team maps out the curriculum to ensure that all the aims and objectives of the state standards are addressed during the year. Sometimes they take a deep look at which students need enrichment or extension and which need extra practice or instruction. Sometimes they share ideas about what assignments to create. As a result of the collaboration, that teacher says she is a "110 percent better teacher" than she was in her previous school.

Once teachers have developed expertise in collaborative meetings, It's Being Done leaders often pull back and go to fewer of them, letting teachers be the experts on their work. But they still go over agendas, minutes, and work products to make sure that the meetings remain focused and high enough quality to ensure that all students are successful. They know that even once a system is in place, the role of a leader is to continually monitor to ensure that it continues to be effective.

Collaboration at the high school level looks somewhat different, in part because of the specialized knowledge required in each subject. "As principal I can't be the school's science specialist," said John Capozzi of Elmont. "I have to rely on my department chairs." Capozzi considers his main job to be that of helping department chairs provide support to their teachers. At Elmont most department chairs teach only two classes so that they have time to provide help and guidance to their teachers. They review lesson plans every week and provide feedback to help ensure that teachers keep their lessons clear, focused, and aimed at having the students grapple with difficult material at a high level.[6] But no teacher is left to teach by him- or herself. All have colleagues to collaborate with, bounce ideas off, and become better with.

DEVELOPING EXPERTISE

Their years of experience mean It's Being Done principals can be confident about what they know will work for students—focusing on standards, curriculum, research-proven teaching methods, and the use of data to drive improvement.

But that doesn't mean that It's Being Done leaders think they have all the answers or even that they should. This is why they encourage and require their teachers to develop deep expertise. A few of the elementary schools, for example, departmentalize their instruction—particularly at the upper grades—so that teachers will be able to explore in a systematic and rigorous way one or two subjects. North Godwin pairs teachers, for example, so that some teach math and science; others English and social studies. But departmentalizing has the downside, particularly in small schools, of reducing the numbers of teachers available for the kind of deep collaboration that is described above. One way of handling this is demonstrated by George Hall, where all teachers teach all subjects, but some teachers have become the experts in science, social studies, and technology, and they are responsible for keeping up with the latest research and materials and making sure that their colleagues are kept abreast of the most important developments and can act as resources for them.

This is part of what It's Being Done principals talk about when they talk of building "teacher leaders." They are anxious to give over appropriate instructional decisions to teachers, allowing the people closest to the issue to decide things such as the right phonics programs, the right math games to use, the right computer programs to order, and so on. They make sure that teachers have the requisite knowledge and skills, and then encourage them to use that knowledge in making decisions.

Debbie Bolden, who helped turn around George Hall Elementary School as assistant principal and is now principal of her own school, said: "I look at myself not as the boss, but one who is able to provide [teachers] with the necessary components it takes to be successful in the classroom. I feel it is important to build teacher leaders in the building."

Many of them are very explicit in encouraging their teachers to try new things and take risks. But they do this within a system of continual monitoring through the review of student performance data in collaborative meetings. That monitoring means that success and failure can both be noticed. Success can be shared, and failure can be noticed and corrected quickly without allowing it to harm students. So, if a teacher thinks a particular math game will help students learn how to convert fractions to decimals but in fact it just served to confuse them, the data reviews ensure that it is noticed quickly and another method is tried.

Veteran teachers unused to looking at data often view the activity with apprehension and suspicion. Studying spreadsheets is not what they expected to do when they trained as teachers.

One veteran North Godwin teacher, for example, said that she was very disconcerted when Arelis Diaz first laid out how she expected teachers to work. Her first response was that she didn't think assessments were "developmentally appropriate" for first grade. "I told her that I had had several principals before her and would no doubt have several principals after her, and I wasn't going to change the way I worked," said Deb Smith recently. Principals attempting to change the traditions of a school or teachers' practice often face this type of opposition.

Diaz recently remembered that initial conversation: "She told me it wasn't developmentally appropriate to look at data. But when I asked her which students were successful and which students were low and why and what we could do about it, she couldn't tell me how her students were doing."

Once Smith saw the value of understanding exactly what students needed to know when they left her classroom and tracking their individual progress through data, she changed her mind. She says she is now one of the most enthusiastic data trackers in the school because she understands that the data help her ensure that each one of her students masters "developmentally appropriate goals for first-graders."

Because the principals in our study were, overall, in classrooms for a long time and have faced all the issues their teachers face, they have great authority in questions of instruction. They can often offer a suggestion to improve classroom management, the organization of materials, time management—the day-to-day problems that every teacher faces.

So, for example, when Barbara Adderley noticed that one class took ten minutes to get books, paper, and writing materials together for a lesson, she suggested to the teacher that he organize the materials in bins that could be placed on the tables ahead of time, cutting down on both the waste of time and the opportunity for students to be mischievous. The teacher later noted how smoothly his classes had been going since he had taken her suggestion.

It's Being Done leaders recognize that many teachers—particularly new teachers—are woefully unprepared to manage a classroom, plan effective lessons, assess whether their students are learning, and figure out what to do if they aren't. They know that teachers new to their schools will need help with all that and more.

So they often make sure they are paired with mentor teachers and have ways of systematically providing help, usually through a careful observation process. Sometimes this is provided by a nonsupervisor, such as an instructional coach; sometimes it is the principal or another administrator. But It's

Being Done leaders make sure that teachers—particularly teachers new to the school—are regularly observed and provided help. At the elementary school level there is a similar recognition that few new teachers have been trained to understand the fundamentals of reading and math instruction. So, for example, Molly Bensinger-Lacy asked new teachers to commit to attending afterschool classes in literacy instruction throughout the school year.

Similarly, Ware Elementary essentially runs its own teacher-preparation program after school. Ware is unusual among established It's Being Done schools in that it still has fairly high teacher turnover rates. In part because it is located on an army base, with all the transience of any military post, teachers rarely stay more than a few years. Gustafson and Black have cultivated a relationship with nearby Kansas State University, which provides many of their student teachers and new teachers, but they don't have years to wait for teachers to improve. They immediately start them with an intensive program teaching them about every aspect of classroom teaching, from establishing a classroom environment of respect to reading, writing, and math instruction.

This is an example of how It's Being Done principals recognize the unique contexts of their schools and the resources they have available and make choices accordingly. For Gustafson and Black, new teacher induction was necessary to accomplish the learning goals they had for their school and students.

MANAGING TEACHERS—HIRING, FIRING, AND OBSERVING

It's Being Done principals tend to give just about all the credit for their schools' improvement to their teachers (see figure 4.3). In fact, 47 percent of them say one of the most important factors in their school's improvement was teachers and instruction. Many of them go even further and say that the classroom is where all the really difficult work gets done. Mary Haynes-Smith, who runs a very demanding school even by It's Being Done school standards, says that being principal is much easier than being a teacher.

So It's Being Done principals are extremely respectful of the knowledge and skills required to be a good teacher and are eager to give teachers credit for any and all improvements. But they are also uncompromising about the

Figure 4.3: What factors have affected improvement in It's Being Done schools?

Source: The Education Trust Principal Survey, Part 3, question 9, and www.wordle.net.

need for every teacher to be a good teacher. "No one has the right to waste a day in the life of a child," says Valarie Lewis, principal of P.S./M.S. 124 in Queens.

For this reason, they focus a lot of attention on who is teaching in their building and do what they can to ensure that they have really good teachers working for them. It's Being Done principals say they have an influence on hiring, but no more so than other principals (see figure 4.4).

Like most averages, this one hides a large range of experience. Some It's Being Done principals, such as Barbara Adderley, Elain Thompson, Tom Graham, and Molly Bensinger-Lacy, inherited an existing staff; others inherited a staff decimated by departures, like Deb Gustafson. Still others were part of a reconstitution, where somewhere between 50 percent and 100 percent of the staff were new. Even those who took over reconstituted schools had a range of experience: Terri Tomlinson was able to hire her staff when she arrived at the reconstituted George Hall Elementary School; Von Sheppard arrived at the reconstituted Dayton's Bluff with the staff already selected by the district. Still others, such as Conrad Lopes at Jack Britt High School, were part of starting an entirely new school and had the opportunity to hire new staff members.

Figure 4.4: Principals' perception of influence over hiring

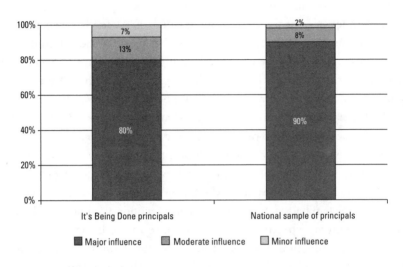

Source: Schools and Staffing Survey, 2007–2008, The Education Trust Principal Survey, Part 1, question 9.

The question arises, then, how It's Being Done principals approach hiring when they have the chance, which most often comes in filling openings in their buildings as people transfer, retire, or leave for some other reason. In short, they view every hire as a key opportunity to help shape the instructional culture of the school.

"I would leave a position open rather than hire the wrong person," said Arelis Diaz, the former principal of North Godwin Elementary School, giving voice to the seriousness all It's Being Done principals feel about hiring.

Depending on their districts, they may have to hire from a preselected pool, but principals usually still have choices to make from within those pools. Some It's Being Done principals say that, especially at the beginning of their tenure, they needed to actively recruit teachers because their schools had such terrible reputations that few teachers would apply. This was true of, for example, Stanton Elementary in Philadelphia and Granger High School in the Yakima Valley of Washington. One story gives a sense of what Adderley had to deal with: A young teacher she had hired straight out of college had been teaching just a short time and was showing promise when her parents came to Philadelphia, packed her up, and moved her out rather than let her continue teaching at Stanton. As for Ricardo Esparza of Granger, he said, "I recruited in grocery stores, anywhere I could." As the schools improved and word spread among teachers that they were good places to work, recruiting became a little easier—though neither Adderley nor Esparza was ever inundated with good candidates. Other schools have had an easier time hiring as their reputations have spread. Elmont, for example, now gets hundred of applicants for every opening.

When they're hiring, It's Being Done principals vary in the external characteristics they look for. Some look for experience; others would rather hire and train brand-new teachers who haven't been inculcated in what they consider to be bad habits. Some (particularly secondary schools) look more closely at content expertise; others look more for pedagogical expertise. Some disdain education degrees; others look for them, but are partial to graduates of particular colleges and universities that they think do a good job training teachers.

Elmont has been at the improvement process long enough that it is now able to hire back some of its graduates, something many of the secondary schools aspire to. They know that former students understand at a deep level the many obstacles their students face and are undaunted by some of the behaviors students exhibit—some of which mirror their own previous behavior. Jason Allen, a social studies teacher at Elmont, for example, loves remembering the ways he and then-football coach and current principal John Capozzi clashed when he was a student. "That made our relationship stronger," Allen said.

All of the leaders in this study look for teachers who are willing to dedicate themselves to the school's mission.

Looking for teachers who will devote themselves to ensuring that all students will succeed means It's Being Done leaders are looking for teachers with what many call a good "work ethic," by which they mean willingness to work hard until a job is done. They want to be sure, for example, that the teacher who agrees to research field trips will do it in a timely fashion; other teachers and students rely on them. They explain to prospective hires that teaching in a high-needs school requires more work than in schools where most of the children are middle-class and have more family resources. They explain what that means: extra tutoring time, extra time collaborating with colleagues and reaching out to families, extra time keeping current with professional literature and developing content expertise, and extra time thinking about what prerequisites are necessary for students to understand a given lesson and how to engage them in learning particular material.

It's important to note that for the most part teachers are paid stipends for extra activities, so they aren't necessarily being asked to work more without compensation. But they are being asked to work more than ordinary teachers are usually required to do, and are often told straight up that that's what is required in a high-needs school. If they don't want to work that hard, they are often told, they should look elsewhere. "This is not a 9–3 job," said Diane Scricca.

Typical questions of potential hires include, "What would you do if half of your students fail a test?" It's Being Done leaders do not want to hear lectures about how kids today are too distracted by video games to study. They want to hear some variation of, "Well, I'd have to go figure out what I need to improve in my instruction." Similarly, when they ask what prospective teachers would do if most kids didn't do their homework, they are looking for some variation of, "Maybe my homework assignment was unclear or boring."

In other words, they are looking for potential teachers to look to their own practices for solutions rather than blaming the students or the students' parents for failure.

It's Being Done leaders are also looking for something a little more indefinable. John Capozzi calls it the "Elmont Heart," and other It's Being Done leaders have similar ways of talking about it. It has to do with a genuine liking of students and desire to develop real relationships with them. "Kids won't learn from people who don't like them," said Diane Scricca, former principal of Elmont.

So when they have the opportunity to hire a teacher, they look for teachers who not only believe that all students can learn but that they can teach all their students. They look for people who know their subject area and like kids. They don't look for perfection but for teachers willing to learn new things in order to get better. It's Being Done Leaders spend a lot of time explaining the mission of the school and the way the school operates to prospective hires. "Before they ever begin here, we explain this is an ongoing learning experience and it should never stop," said Capozzi.

In keeping with the collaborative nature of their schools, It's Being Done principals often make hiring a collaborative process. So, for example, at Roxbury Prep Charter School, prospective teachers are expected to teach a lesson to a class with other teachers observing, listen to their feedback, and then re-teach the lesson incorporating the suggestions they were given. This process ensures that teachers unable to work in collaborative ways or unable to react constructively to critiques will be identified before hiring.

Each of the It's Being Done leaders handles this a little differently, but most have some kind of process to ensure that teachers have a say in the hiring of their colleagues. "It's been many years since I hired someone without input from the rest of the staff," said Molly Bensinger-Lacy shortly after she retired.

This is partly a recognition that teachers should be able to have some say in who they will be working closely with. After all, they will be relying on these teachers for research, lesson planning, help learning new skills, and on and on. They don't have to be best friends, but they do need to respect and rely on their colleagues. It is also a recognition that teachers can be keen observers of their colleagues. "They ask much harder questions than I do," said Dana Lehman, former codirector of Roxbury Preparatory School.

Not all have such an inclusive process, however. At the large comprehensive high schools in our study—Elmont and Jack Britt—principals see hiring as a job for administrators. "The department chairs recommend four possibilities and then I meet with them," said John Capozzi of Elmont. Similarly, Conrad Lopes of Jack Britt said, "Hiring is strictly an administrative job because teachers don't necessarily know what we're looking for."

Many times It's Being Done leaders consciously use the process of taking on student teachers or hiring paraprofessionals or teacher aides as a way to try out a potential teacher, and they watch closely to see if they would make a good teacher.

But even when a teacher is offered the first contract, that is not the end of the hiring process. Most It's Being Done leaders consider the first few years to be an extended interview during which they are looking for growth, development, and commitment. If, after the first year or second, a new teacher is not what one school calls a "superstar," he or she is let go before they gain tenure protections.

This is in direct contrast to many schools where, if teachers don't do anything terrible, they tend to continue teaching. Their third or fourth contract, when tenure protections take effect, requires no special demonstration of competence in many schools. That is not true in It's Being Done schools. "No one drifts into tenure at Elmont," said John Capozzi.

It's Being Done leaders also work hard to ensure that teachers are in the right spots to be most successful. Before she ever walked through Stanton's doors, Adderley looked at the attendance records of the teaching staff and noted who was frequently absent on Mondays and Fridays and who was in school every day, thus demonstrating what she called a "commitment" to the school and the students. Two teachers who she noted were always in school were fifth-grade teacher Christina Taylor and kindergarten teacher Kathleen Shallow. Watching them convinced her they should be instructional leaders. Taylor became the math instructional coach and Shallow the literacy coach, and she put them in charge of making sure teachers fully understood the content and the relevant teaching methods. One important thing to note is that many schools—particularly schools with federal Title I funds—have positions like reading and math coaches, but not all use those positions as carefully as Adderley did. For example, in many schools the coaches end up serving in large part as floating substitute teachers and filling in whenever there is a need for another pair of hands, such as tutoring individual students or small groups of students. Adderley insisted that Taylor and Shallow were teachers of teachers, not students. The only time they taught students was as part of a model lesson to demonstrate to teachers the kinds of things they could be doing. In this way, Taylor and Shallow helped improve all the instruction in the building rather than helping only a few students.

Similarly, Molly Bensinger-Lacy tapped Kate O'Donnell and Aileen Flaherty as instructional leaders and pulled them from classrooms to help other teachers improve their instruction.

It's Being Done leaders also pay particular attention to classroom assignments and will often reassign teachers who may not have been successful at one grade level to another to try to match their personality and skill with the appropriate level of class. Sometimes they find that teachers who aren't successful managing a full class are still excellent at helping small groups of students catch up and will assign them as "interventionists," helping individual students or small groups of students catch up.

They are also adamant that their best teachers teach the kids who need the most help. "We took our best teachers and put them in the remedial classes," said Conrad Lopes, the founding principal of Jack Britt High School. Many teachers consider it a punishment to teach what they call the "low" kids, such as kids repeating algebra in ninth or tenth grade. These are the students whose knowledge and skills have been identified as below where they should be, and students who see themselves as failures often pose the biggest discipline and academic problems. But Jack Britt and the other It's Being Done leaders specifically look for teachers who will not look at such assignments as punishment but as an honor and a leadership position. For example, one of Elmont's most skilled English teachers, Wendy Tague, has been teaching Read 180 classes to seventh- and eighth-graders for the past few years.[7] Some teachers with her level of enthusiasm for teaching literature would chafe at teaching basic reading skills to students who arrive at school reading below grade level. She has embraced the task with enthusiasm, making sure that all parts of the program work together with New York's English Language Arts standards, and she is thrilled at introducing serious literature to students who were unsuccessful readers until they arrived in her classroom. "I love it," she said.

Paying attention to the quality of teaching means that It's Being Done principals must be clear-eyed about confronting inadequate instruction. "It's the job of a principal to make a marginal teacher uncomfortable," said Jennie Black, assistant principal of Ware Elementary.

Again, each It's Being Done leader has a slightly different way of approaching this question, but one of the hallmarks of It's Being Done principals is that they try not to base their judgments on personal feelings.

A dramatic example of this comes from Barbara Adderley. When she arrived at Stanton Elementary, she found a very demoralized school. The staff clearly had few expectations that she would be anything more than another drive-by principal like the ones who had preceded her. In her first meeting with the faculty, one teacher angrily said to her, "You think you're going to fix us? We're going to fix you!" Adderley said that she simply sat back and smiled to herself, saying, "Well, you're first on my list."

A boss of any sort would see such open defiance as a problem and might well take measures to get rid of or otherwise marginalize that person. But, Adderley said, "I went into her classroom and saw that she was a really good teacher." So, even though many principals would have continued to see that teacher as an enemy, Adderley said she did what she could to support her and make her a leader within the school. "I was really sorry when she retired a few years later."

This ability to filter out personal distractions is key. George Hall Elementary's Terri Tomlinson, for example, says when she was a teacher she maintained a very calm and orderly classroom, and that's her deep preference. But if a teacher is getting really good results with a disorderly classroom, she doesn't question the methods. "It isn't personal," Tomlinson said. "It's business."

The way Tomlinson and other It's Being Done principals make sure they don't let their personal preferences cloud their professional judgment is through data. Data let them know how much progress is being made in each classroom, and lets them see if a teacher is succeeding or failing with her students. "The principal must hold teachers accountable," is the way Arelis Diaz put it.

This can be a very uncomfortable process for teachers whose students are not learning much.

Deb Gustafson and Jennie Black of Ware Elementary say they approach every teacher with the assumption that he or she wants to be successful. To go over data month after month that demonstrates that your students are not meeting standards is discouraging, and developing plans of improvement both for the students and for themselves is time-consuming for teachers. "We'll keep doing it as long as they want to do it," Gustafson said. "But at some point I'll say, 'Wouldn't you be more successful at Dillard's?'" referring to the department store. In this way, they have counseled several teachers out of the profession.

Arelis Diaz said that as principal and, later, assistant superintendent, she would regularly observe and evaluate every teacher whose students were not doing well. "The union would ask me when I would stop evaluating, and I would say, 'When I see better data with evidence that students are learning.'"

At some point, many It's Being Done principals have faced the issue of needing to fire a teacher, although they are more often likely to talk about teachers leaving on their own. Many ordinary principals complain that it is impossible to fire a tenured teacher, particularly in unionized schools, but that's not how It's Being Done principals talk. "You document," said Barbara Adderley, explaining how it is possible to fire a tenured teacher in a highly unionized environment. Teachers who are late, who leave early, who miss trainings, can all be written up and, eventually, dismissed for cause, she said. When Molly Bensinger-Lacy required teachers to attend a training on math instruction and several of her more obdurate teachers did not attend, she was able to document that and thereby begin the process of removing those who continued to shirk their professional responsibilities or failed to do what was necessary to provide a high-quality learning program for students.

Elain Thompson of P.S./M.S. 124 in Queens says that truly bad teachers almost always provide the opportunity for diligent principals to dismiss them. Shortly after her retirement, Thompson said that Lewis was despairing of getting rid of a teacher she considered particularly bad. Thompson told her that no doubt he would provide an opening, and made it her business to pass by his classroom on her frequent visits to the school. One day she saw that he had gone down the hall, leaving his class without an adult in charge. "I wrote him up and he was gone," Thompson said.

Rarely talked about in the field of education is how unwilling many principals are to confront teachers and document their failings with clear evidence. When asked in national surveys, principals often say they would like more power to fire teachers, but it is clear from the data that too many of them aren't doing the very basic management functions that would allow them to know who is doing a good job with whom and how.[8] Even when teachers don't put in a full day's work, don't plan lessons to take up all the instructional time, or show movies, many principals don't interfere.

A principal of our acquaintance in a diverse suburban school says he believes he is treating teachers "as professionals" when he watches them leave day after day before the contractual end of the day because he doesn't believe in interfering with how they carry out their responsibilities.

That isn't how It's Being Done principals think. They see themselves as the guardians of their students' futures, and they understand that proper use of time is the absolute key to their students getting an education. As such they are resolute in making sure that teachers are putting in the hours necessary. Molly Bensinger-Lacy has said she thinks many principals are unwilling to play that management role in part because it is very uncomfortable and makes principals unpopular—at least initially, when new expectations are being put in place. When she arrived at Graham Road, which then had a year-round schedule that started in early August, teachers had been used to taking time off during the first month of school to go on family vacations, attend family reunions, or to work in summer camps. When she said they could no longer do that, teachers became angry. Few educators like to be the bad guy, and Bensinger-Lacy said she had to remind herself that she was safeguarding the futures of the students, not the happiness of the teachers.

Making sure that every teacher understands that every day of instruction is precious and not to be squandered is one way that It's Being Done principals convey the urgency of the mission of the school, but it also means that many teachers unwilling to work hard have a tendency to weed themselves out. Many It's Being Done principals report that they saw an exodus of teachers after their first year, which allowed them to hire replacements who were willing to dedicate themselves to the school mission of success for each child. Once the schools are fully functional, with collaborative teams in place and working well, teachers often take on the role of making uncooperative teachers uncomfortable. "Good teachers will force the bad ones out," said Von Sheppard.

That doesn't mean that It's Being Done principals, particularly those in unionized schools, don't sometimes grumble and complain about the difficulties in firing bad teachers. But most say they were able to when they needed to.

It's Being Done principals understand that they run challenging schools. A teacher who would be good enough in a middle-class school simply isn't good enough in a high-needs school. And so they will often encourage teachers who are not performing up to their standards to find positions they might be better suited for in other types of schools. Valarie Lewis says she actively helps marginal teachers find jobs in less demanding schools.

Ricardo Esparza had a little speech he used whenever a teacher balked at doing the kinds of things Esparza wanted: "You're a great teacher, but we have a different philosophy. I'd be happy to write you a letter of recommendation." He was able to encourage a number of teachers to leave that way.

But, as Barbara Adderley said, summing up what all It's Being Done principals think, "It isn't just about hiring and firing. It's about developing teachers."

CONCLUSION

It's Being Done leaders demonstrate how it is possible for principals to be the "instructional leaders" of schools. They do this not by making all the instructional decisions but by helping their teachers work together to develop the deep expertise in both the content and pedagogy necessary to be able to make the myriad instructional decisions that take place every hour of every school day. The one role they never give over, however, is in setting performance standards. They expect every student to be academically successful and never compromise that goal. They recognize the difficulties many of their students face in meeting academic goals. But they see academic success as the way out of poverty and isolation, and are determined to make sure their students have a chance at better lives in the future.

CHAPTER FIVE

The Job That Never Goes Away

Managing the Building

It is all well and good to say that It's Being Done leaders are "instructional" leaders, but many principals around the country will say in response, "Where do they find the time?" This is not irrational. All principals have myriad responsibilities. Teacher observations, collaboration and data meetings, and even contractually required teacher evaluations are often experienced as chores tacked on to an already unwieldy to-do list.

A quick story illustrates the problem. A deputy state superintendent of our acquaintance once told of a high-level meeting where elementary principals from all over the state were being given new information about the state's standards and assessments. Deep into substantive discussions of alignment, instruction, and best practices, the meeting was interrupted for twenty minutes for the principals to learn how to fold lunchroom tables without breaking a finger. That encapsulates the job of principal: high-level intellectual demands coupled with excruciatingly detailed tasks of varied levels and importance, many of which concern the safety and well-being of children and staff. "I don't know how anybody does this job," said the deputy superintendent.

There is no question that the job will always be complex and time-consuming. "You're running a major enterprise," is the way Diane Scricca of Elmont puts it. To make the job doable, however, our high performing leaders make sure their managerial responsibilities do double duty—not only do they ensure that the building runs smoothly, but they also serve the instructional focus of the school. In this chapter we will share how the principals reframe typical responsibilities such as the school schedule, discipline policies, and school improvement teams to serve the academic mission of the school and how their role changes over time.

ALLOCATING TIME AND ATTENTION

The first question in this regard has to do with how principals spend their own time. Although we don't have perfectly comparable information on how It's Being Done principals compare to other principals, one study in the Miami-Dade school district may be instructive.[1] In that study, researchers followed principals around for a full day and recorded what they did every five minutes. After eliminating transition and personal time, they found that the principals in the study spent about one-third of their time on administration, which the researchers defined as fulfilling compliance requirements including special education regulations, managing school schedules, discipline, attendance, and student services. They spent another quarter of their time on "organizational management," which the researchers defined as managing the budget, hiring, networking with other principals, and other similar activities. They spent only about 15 percent of their time on the instructional program and day-to-day instruction such as coaching teachers, using data to improve instruction, planning afterschool activities, and talking with students

The highly effective principals in our study report spending their time very differently. When asked to assign percentages of time to the same six categories the Miami-Dade principals' activities were placed into, they said they spend almost half of their time on the instructional program and day-to-day instruction and only a little more than a quarter of their time on administration and organizational management. Both groups of principals spend about the same amount of time on internal and external relations (see figure 5.1).

We have to be cautious about making direct comparisons between the two groups, because no one was recording the It's Being Done leaders. On any given day they could look like the Miami-Dade principals. But their responses reflect how they ideally want and plan to spend their time. They try to keep from being distracted from their instructional focus by the

Figure 5.1: How principals distribute their time

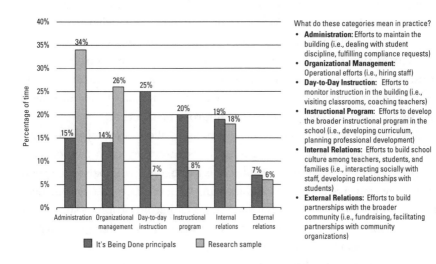

Source: The Education Trust Principal Survey, Part 1; E. L. Horng, D. Klasik, & S. Loeb, *Principal Time-Use and School Effectiveness,* CALDER Working Paper 34 (Washington, DC, Urban Institute, 2009).

kinds of activities that take up a lot of time of many principals. Interestingly, the research from the Miami-Dade study found that principals in higher-performing schools were more likely to spend their time on day-to-day instruction whereas principals in lower-performing schools spent more of their time on administration, demonstrating the potential impact of these choices.

It's Being Done principals ensure that they don't get distracted by scheduling their time to reflect their instructional priorities. So, for example, they make sure that the first things they schedule are observation of instruction, data meetings, leadership meetings, and the other core activities key to improving instruction. Other things are fitted in once those responsibilities are fulfilled. As Valarie Lewis of P.S./M.S. 124 said, "I have a plan at the beginning of every day that I try not to stray far from." Similarly, Sheri Shirley of Oakland Heights Elementary said, "I make a list of things I have to do every day, and I always put the instructional items first."

In this way, they avoid what Sharon Brittingham of Frankford Elementary calls "majoring in the minors." Brittingham has spent the years since retiring from Frankford working with principals around Delaware, and she has found that many principals allow their time to be taken up with the daily crises that emerge in any school—the cafeteria runs out of French fries, the green bus is late, the music teacher is sick, the bathroom ceiling leaks. The list is endless and can easily eat up a principal's time until there is little time left for those things that improve instruction.

Brittingham speculates that many principals allow themselves to focus on these kinds of quick-win problems because they earn school-wide approbation for being indispensible crisis managers. Principals who spend their time visiting classrooms and meeting with teachers to examine data are not likely to be greeted by their staffs as heroic problem-solvers, at least initially, and Brittingham thinks that wanting to be liked plays a part in how many principals spend their time.

It's Being Done leaders have a normal wish to be liked, but they don't let that deflect them from their professional responsibilities and personal accountability for student learning. They have high expectations for their schools and teachers, and they know if they aren't achieving their goals, ultimately, it is their responsibility.

EVERY ADULT PLAYS A CRITICAL ROLE

Of course, the daily crises of school life need to be handled. But, as Elain Thompson of P.S. 124 said, when asked how she kept them from distracting her, "That's someone else's job." She went on to say that it wasn't her job to solve all the problems in a school. It was her job to ensure that there were competent people in every position in the school able to solve problems.

For that reason, It's Being Done leaders bring the same kind of rigor to hiring and monitoring the work of custodians, secretaries, and cafeteria workers as they do to hiring teachers and teacher aides.

"Most principals don't understand that the support staff can be your undertakers," Tomlinson said. "They can bury you." They can also help you be successful, and the principals expect all staff members not only to be part of creating a culture and climate of excellence but also to take on significant day-to-day problem-solving responsibilities key to running the building. In the same way that they work to empower teachers to make instructional decisions while retaining the role of setting performance standards, It's Being Done leaders empower support staff to solve day-to-day problems. They never abandon the support, monitoring, and evaluative role that rests with the principal, but they expect staff members to have or develop the expertise necessary to do their jobs.

This is something that takes time. Most of the leaders reflected that they had to be involved in more of the decisions early on but that they intentionally worked to build the capacity of all the staff in their school so that they could reapportion responsibility over time.

But there is something even more profound about the way these leaders manage their buildings: their mission of ensuring that every student is successful is part of everything they do. It is the basis of every decision they make and permeates even seemingly mundane responsibilities. Ultimately, what that means is that none of their responsibilities is mundane. Each is critical and each serves the larger purpose of improving student achievement.

As a result, even the time It's Being Done leaders spend on what is considered to be "administration" and "organizational management" is really about helping students succeed academically.

BUILDING A MASTER SCHEDULE

Scheduling is the quintessential administrative task. Making sure students and staff have someplace to be at all times is a logistical puzzle. Even small schools pose a challenge; big schools can be nightmarish.

It's Being Done leaders don't see it that way, however—or, at least, they don't see it *only* that way.

They begin by seeing time as a resource in short supply. They know that their students need every minute of instructional time that can be eked out of the school day. In addition, they know that teachers need time away from their students to collaborate. Scheduling is the way to make both happen. By making it a lever to move student achievement, they transform the task of scheduling from a mechanistic chore, filling time blocks and rooms with teachers and students, into a key instructional improvement strategy.

Let's look at what that means, first in elementary and middle schools and then at the high school level. Up through eighth grade, principals' key scheduling and assignment responsibilities have to do with building class rosters, assigning teachers and teacher aides, and scheduling lunch, recess, and the "specials." Specials vary from school to school, depending on the district, but generally include art, music, physical education, computer, and sometimes science or social studies at the elementary level, or "technical arts" at the middle school level.

The leaders think of specials as being an important part of education in their own right, but they also schedule them to ensure that classroom teachers are able to use the time their students are in specials productively. So, for example, until Arelis Diaz became principal of North Godwin, the specials teachers had drawn up their own schedule and, she said, had done it based pretty much on which classes they felt like teaching when. Diaz allowed them to continue drawing up the schedule, "but I gave them parameters," she said. "I told them that they needed to teach in such a way that all the grade levels had common planning time."

That small change meant that suddenly classroom teachers had regular times they could collaborate with colleagues at the same grade level during the school day. Scheduling specials in this way is a common strategy among the leaders who believe that collaboration is at the core of school improvement. University Park Campus School, which has middle as well as high school grades, and Roxbury Preparatory Charter School, which is a middle school, have the advantage and disadvantage of being very small. The advantage of only having about two hundred students is that each teacher "owns" a subject at a grade level and is sure of teaching every student in the building at some point. The disadvantage is that they don't have colleagues who are teaching the same subject at the same grade to collaborate with. Roxbury Prep addresses this issue by developing "inquiry teams" so that, for example, the math and science teachers, across grades, might collaborate on how to teach measurement, which is a topic that arises in both subjects. University Park Campus School takes a whole-school approach and, during their common planning time, study school-wide data and make key decisions for the whole school.

At Port Chester Middle School, Carmen Macchia scheduled specials (called electives) in such a way that the middle school teams—each of which were responsible for roughly 120 students—met once a day for a full class period. Each team had slightly different ways of doing things, but often three days a week they talked about curriculum, assessment, cross-disciplinary lessons, and data, leaving two days a week for the team to discuss problems with individual students, bringing in the student, the student's family members, the counselor, social worker, and anyone else needed.

At Graham Road Elementary, additional time for collaboration was carved out by having teacher aides begin the morning for one grade level per day. So, for example, the first-grade team of teachers would begin meeting one day a week at the beginning of the contractual day, 15 minutes before school started. They would continue for 45 minutes after school began, one week talking about reading, the next about math. In addition to the classroom teachers, the English for Speakers of Other Languages (ESOL) teacher for that grade would be there, as would the special educator assigned to first grade and either the reading or math instructional coach. One strategy that they used to make the most of this time was to have one teacher present findings from a major piece of research; after a brief discussion, the group would work on some way to put the finding into practice, producing the actual classroom materials that they would use. Meanwhile, the teacher aides would settle students into their classrooms, collecting homework and lunch money and starting on plans left by teachers.

In the two Delaware schools, Gary Brittingham and Sharon Brittingham also saw the beginning of school as a crucial time, but they used it for the individual tutoring of students. Students who needed to be caught up or re-taught would be alerted the day before that they should rush off the bus, grab their food, and have a working breakfast with teachers for twenty minutes while their classmates had a more leisurely and social breakfast in the cafeteria. Another variation on this same theme was that Barbara Adderley had breakfast delivered to classrooms so that all students had "working breakfasts" during which teachers would often read aloud to the students while they ate.

All these examples show the way It's Being Done leaders battle anything that resembled a waste of time. They rethink every use of time and make sure it is used for the benefit of students. Each principal manages this a little differently depending on their size, needs of students, and available teaching staff, but they made the changes they felt were necessary even if it meant questioning long tradition.

For example, when Deb Gustafson arrived at Ware Elementary she found that teachers had worked out among themselves a schedule so that each class had a fifteen-minute block in the morning and afternoon to go en masse to the bathroom. "Half-an-hour of instructional time spent going to the bathroom every day!" she remembered indignantly. "Not to mention the fact that children don't all have to go on the same schedule!" She ended that practice, and today students slip quietly out of class when they need to.

This demonstrates how principals help set a new culture by changing established routines.

Time wasting in schools, it should be noted, is not a trivial issue. A large national study led by Robert Pianta for the National Institute of Child Health and Human Development found that 17 percent of instructional time in fifth-grade classrooms was spent "managing time and materials"—in other words, almost one-fifth of instructional time was wasted by fussing with overhead projectors or laptop computers, handing out books, and collecting homework papers.[2]

In addition, Pianta's researchers found vast amounts of instructional time were taken up with low-level basic skills, often through the use of worksheets, rather than more complex problem-solving or other higher-level instruction. It's Being Done leaders are determined that no instructional time be wasted because of bad scheduling, but they are equally adamant that the time teachers spend with students must be focused on rigorous, challenging activities. As discussed in chapter 3, the principals' vision for student success didn't just include mastery of the basics; rather, it included problem solving and application of knowledge. One scheduling strategy used by some of the elementary principals to encourage challenging and engaging instruction for all students is to schedule instruction so that all students in a particular grade level—sometimes even in the entire school—are working on the same subjects at the same time. Some of the schools use the common instructional time to "regroup" their students so that they are in homogenous groupings for those subjects.

Other schools keep their heterogeneous (mixed-ability) homerooms together but provide for individualized instruction by providing "center activities" for students to work independently or in small groups on math games, reading, writing, working on the computer, or some other activity while teachers work with small groups and individual students.

Those times are often when teacher aides, instructional specialists, teachers of English as a second language, and special educators come into classrooms to work with individual students or small groups of students, providing additional support to the classroom teacher and more opportunity to tailor instruction for each student.

During her first week as principal, Molly Bensinger-Lacy provided teachers with a master schedule that laid out specific blocks of time for math, language arts, science, social studies, and specials (music, physical education, art, library, counseling, computer lab, and Spanish) for each grade level. "Teachers were to adhere strictly to the instructional blocks because that was when resource teachers would be coming into their classrooms to teach small guided reading or math groups," she said. This was a change for the teachers, but was nonnegotiable and was a way to demonstrate priorities and organize the instruction necessary for students.

In order to establish the kinds of classroom routines that permit teachers to work with small groups while other students work on their own, teachers often have to spend time in the beginning of the year making sure students understand how to work independently in small groups or by themselves. "I told my teachers to do nothing but establish classroom routines for the first three weeks," said Molly Bensinger-Lacy, adding that those three weeks meant the rest of the year could be much more productive once every student understood exactly what was expected throughout the day.

Another example is illustrated by North Godwin. When Arelis Diaz became principal, she inherited a Reading Recovery Program with one teacher and three teacher aides. Reading Recovery is a program that has documented considerable success with many students and provides valuable training for teachers.[3] However, it is very expensive and time-consuming. Each adult works with one struggling first-grade student at a time for thirty minutes for between twelve and twenty weeks. "They were working with a minimal number of students, compared to the number of students who needed help," Diaz said.

Diaz offered her kindergarten and first-grade teachers the opportunity to have the Reading Recovery team come into their classrooms during the literacy block to work with individual students and small groups. "They couldn't turn that down," Diaz said. The Reading Recovery team used the same techniques they had been using for individual students, but were able to reach far more students by swooping in as a team and working with small groups of students.

As a result, by midyear, Diaz said, more than 50 percent of the first-graders were reading independently. "That process was a huge victory because the teachers loved it," she said. "Teachers . . . were seeing their kids zoom through these levels that had taken them a whole year to get through. Every teacher loves to see students learning—that's why we go into teaching. And when it was happening at such a consistent level throughout the building, it was exciting."

This last story illustrates another aspect of It's Being Done leadership, which is that the leaders take stock of all the programs and resources in their schools and make sure they are serving the school and students' needs. Reading Recovery is a program designed for schools that have relatively few first-grade students who are having difficulty in reading. At North Godwin many of the children arrive speaking little or no English, and most of the first-graders could be seen as struggling readers. In such a situation, it was simply inadequate to the task. By incorporating the training and resources it provided into classroom instruction, Diaz both improved students' reading and reduced the number of programs she needed to monitor. At this point, many high-poverty and high-minority schools are awash in programs and resources that sometimes work at cross purposes. Like Diaz, all It's Being Done leaders work to ensure that whatever programs they have work together to improve student achievement and jettison anything that isn't helpful.

Another piece of elementary school scheduling is building class rosters. Some It's Being Done leaders keep that chore for themselves; others turn it over to the teachers with guidelines, which has the effect both of building teamwork among teachers and empowering them to make key instructional decisions. Even then, however, principals continue to review the class rosters to make sure teachers have met whatever guidelines the principal set for gender balance, skill-level balance, and so forth. This is not a strategy to lessen the workload of the principal, but rather to put decisions appropriate to classroom teachers in their hands. This is also not simply allowing teachers to pick and choose the students they want to teach or letting senior teachers have their pick of the crop but making sure that teachers make important decisions about student achievement. The principal must help build teachers' skills so that teachers are making choices that put the needs of the students first and support the teaching and learning goals for the school.

HIGH SCHOOL SCHEDULES

Scheduling at the high school level poses different challenges from elementary and middle school grades, in part because for the first time students must accumulate credits toward graduation, and in part because it is more difficult to provide common planning times for teachers who teach the same class, much less across a whole department. Leaders must often come up with creative solutions for their schools.

Because Jack Britt High School has a four-by-four block schedule, meaning that students take only four classes a semester, each one lasting ninety minutes a day, principal Denise Garison doesn't even try to provide common planning times for teachers. "We can't have all the Algebra I teachers have planning time at the same time because it means an entire block when students wouldn't be taking Algebra I, which is impossible," she said. So, instead of scheduling ongoing collaborative time during the year, Jack Britt teachers meet for a week before school starts for intensive sessions to study the previous year's scores on end-of-course exams to see where their strengths and weaknesses were, once again study the state's standards, map out curriculum, develop assessments and lesson plans, and look at individual data on incoming students to understand what topics they can review quickly and what topics they will have to start from the beginning.

The practice of collaboration begins in the summer. To foster ongoing talk and discussion, Garison physically clusters the classrooms of teachers who teach the same class together on the same hall. That way, teachers are able to do quick consultations about how students did on a particular assessment or how a particular lesson went before school, after school, and between classes when they are in the hallway. She had clustered key classes—English 9 and Algebra I, for example. But when Jack Britt's test scores on the high school civics exam were not as good as Garison thought they should be, she reassigned classrooms to ensure that all the civics teachers were near one another as well.

Informal hallway consultations are possible because all teachers are expected to be outside their classrooms ten minutes before school starts and between classes, and it is the job of administrators to walk the halls making sure that teachers are at their posts. This policy means that all teachers see their colleagues and supervisors several times throughout the day, which is intended to help create a collegial environment and reduce isolation as well as provide a calming adult presence in the hallways. In exchange for that requirement, no teacher is ever expected to "do lunch duty" as they are in other neighboring high schools. Administrators "cover" each of the four scheduled lunches, meaning that they are in the lunchroom for about two hours a day supervising students, which in turn helps them to know and have relationships with students. "Teachers need lunch," Garison said flatly. Teachers say they often use lunchtime for informal teacher collaboration and conversations about instruction, but this is at their own discretion.

As can be seen from this example, leaders are often faced with competing priorities. Garison understands that she has limited hours in the day to create the structured collaboration that she knows is necessary to reach her equity and excellence goals—but she also knows that teachers need some down time.

To build her master schedule, Garison begins with her staff allotment from the district and then builds a wish list for each of her classes—for example, she knows that students in Algebra I in ninth grade have a lot of ground to make up, so she "wishes" that she can have class sizes of no bigger than eighteen. Advanced placement English can handle bigger classes, so she might "wish" for between twenty-five and twenty-eight. She also asks teachers what they would like to teach. As we saw in chapter 4, Jack Britt hires teachers who are passionate about all students succeeding, so, Garison said, many of her best teachers ask to teach ninth-grade classes, where many of the students enter below grade level.

With student choices, teacher choices, and her wish list for class size entered, the computer program generates a tentative master schedule sometime in early spring. Assistant principals then go through and make adjustments based on actual enrollment, and Garison spends a big chunk of time over the summer personally going through every student's schedule, making sure students and teachers are in the right classes.

One of the things Garison and the administrators ensure is that students don't take two academic classes at the same time that they've struggled with in the past. So, for example, if a student is strong in English and history but weak in math and science, she makes sure that they take only math or science in one semester, with the other class being English or social studies. Knowing that electives are often the classes that most immediately engage struggling students and provide more immediate ways to be successful, she urges students to choose their electives carefully and then works to ensure they get them. She also ensures that the most effective teachers teach the students who most need good instruction.

As a result of all that work over the summer, "Every student has a working schedule on the first day of school," Garison says proudly.

To people who haven't spent much time in high schools, that may seem an odd boast. Why wouldn't students have working schedules on the first day of school? But many high schools have lines of students in the hallways outside counseling offices for the first few days of school with dozens, sometimes hundreds, of students reporting that they are signed up for Algebra I when they should be in Algebra II, or some other similar problem. As a result, high school teachers throughout the country complain of working hard to develop an engaging way to start the year only to have several students slip out and several more slide in the second or third day of school, because of incorrect schedules. "I hated when that happened," Garison said of her years teaching math before coming to Jack Britt. "You work hard to create a community and then students leave and come, and you have to start all over."

Even worse are the many students who reach their senior year without having accumulated the right credits needed for graduation because no adult in the building paid enough attention to their course schedules. This is bad enough when it is unavoidable, such as when students move from districts with different requirements. Garison—and other It's Being Done leaders—consider it inexcusable when it is the result of factors in the school's control.

Many times scheduling problems are caused because high school principals see scheduling as too tedious and complicated and provide little supervision to the counseling department or an assistant principal to whom they assign the task.

"This may go against what people may think is right, but the principal needs to have a hand in scheduling," said Conrad Lopes, Garison's predecessor. "Our administration goes through every single schedule. We make sure that students have met all their prerequisites. It's the administration's responsibility to do this. This way, we know which students are at risk and how we can help them be successful."

Of course, this means less time for something else, but student success is at the heart of these schools, and if students and teachers aren't scheduled in a way to increase student success, then the other tasks of a principal must take a back seat.

At Imperial High School, Lisa Tabarez brought the same sensibility to the issue, "hand scheduling" every student and every class, ensuring that no student drifted through school without having met the state's requirements. She went further and automatically scheduled every student into the college preparatory classes known in California as A-G. Students needed permission to opt out of A-G to be in a less rigorous program, something she actively discouraged. This was part of building the culture of college-going meant that after she had been principal for several years, most Imperial students enrolled in either a two- or four-year college immediately upon graduating.

At Elmont, with two thousand students in grades 7–12 and a nine-period day, scheduling is handled by assistant principal Brian Burke, who takes seriously the need to do what might be called "schedule for success." The middle school grades are "teamed," meaning that a team of teachers has responsibility for about one hundred students throughout the subjects, and teachers follow students from seventh to eighth grade and then loop back to seventh to pick up a new group of students. This process of "looping" means that students and teachers develop much deeper relationships, relationships that are often sustained through the high school years. But Elmont, like Jack Britt, also requires that teachers be in the hall between classes, greeting students and establishing an adult presence. Many quick "How's your baby sister doing?" conversations are conducted as students pass through the hall, making what could be a large, impersonal school feel much more intimate and friendly.

One thing that helps with scheduling at Elmont is that the high school classes are taught at only two levels: Regents (college-preparatory) and advanced, such as Advanced Placement classes. When Diane Scricca first arrived at Elmont, there were those two levels plus regular and "modified," which was remedial. "You looked in the classes and the white kids were in the advanced classes and the black kids were in the modified. I got rid of the modified classes year by year." To do this required extensive professional development. "Teachers were brought up through the tracking system themselves," she said, and they "thought it was the best way to teach kids, and truly did not know how to differentiate instruction within their classrooms." She argues that struggling students should not be grouped together because they need academically successful students to learn from, so this was the first lesson she wanted her staff to learn. To help them understand how ineffective tracking is for students, the faculty read Jeannie Oakes's work.[4] They also made visits to other schools that did not use tracking to see firsthand how they taught diverse groups of students and to hear the benefits from actual colleagues. In addition, they reviewed their own data, particularly from the remedial classes. This allowed them to see that just teaching the same material over and over again did not yield better results for students. Finally, professional development time at the school focused on helping faculty to learn how to diversify their instructional practices to engage students in different ways.

Having four levels of classes adds endless logistical issues in scheduling, and by limiting the course offerings Scricca made Elmont much more educationally equitable, her goal and vision for the school, and ended up simplifying the process of scheduling—but, again, there was an initial investment of her time in helping her teachers learn how to teach in the new environment.

To sum up, It's Being Done leaders see scheduling as not just an administrative task but a key lever for creating adult collaboration and ensuring that students have a successful experience in school. This same attitude can be seen in the way they approach other fundamental tasks that all principals have.

DISCIPLINE POLICIES AND PRACTICES

It's Being Done leaders think of discipline as part of the larger issue of culture and climate, which is a topic dealt with separately in chapter 6. But we deal with it here as well because it is such an integral part of managing the building and maintaining a safe environment.

Every principal in the country could easily spend a great deal of time dealing with students whose behavior ranges from not turning in their homework to fighting. Some principals' offices fill up with students whose teachers have simply tired of them forgetting a pencil and think a talk with the principal will help—or will at least give them a break from each other.

It's Being Done leaders have a guiding principle, which is that instructional time is—to use a word common among them—"sacred." They are explicit with teachers that they must figure out ways to ensure that students do not lose instructional time for petty reasons such as forgetting a pencil. Barbara Adderley of Stanton said she always bought her teachers "lots of pencils—because I never wanted to hear any teacher fuss with a child about a doggone pencil."

But they also know that some of their students live in difficult circumstances, sometimes with people who do not know how to help children control their emotions, and that teachers need help and support in managing behavior. These leaders consider it part of the job of the school as a whole to help students learn how to act in a school setting, which reflects their broader goals for students, as discussed in chapter 3. In this section, we examine how these principals develop systems that don't just meet safety needs but promote healthy learning environments.

Most of the principals spend a fair amount of time in the beginning of their tenure establishing the right discipline policies and routines. In many ways, this is analogous to Molly Bensinger-Lacy's advice to teachers to spend three weeks establishing classroom routines. Routines take time to establish, but once they are established, instruction can proceed without a lot of interruptions. Students know what to expect and so do teachers, and that consistency means that uncertainty doesn't use up precious time and energy. Said Von Sheppard of Dayton's Bluff: "A principal must create an environment where teachers can teach, and students can learn. I don't care how good your teachers are, if they don't feel good about coming to work, if they can't teach without being constantly interrupted, that school is going to have some problems before too long. That's why the visibility of the principal in all classrooms in those first couple of weeks when school begins is crucial. It sets the tone for the rest of the year."

Sometimes It's Being Done leaders establish homegrown discipline policies, sometimes they bring in an outside program. Many use programs with terms like "responsive discipline" or "positive behavioral support," and establish a respectful climate that actively promotes cooperative and helpful behavior while developing logical consequences for disruptive behavior.

At Dayton's Bluff, Von Sheppard encountered what he called the "wild wild west," where students and parents roamed the halls and fights were common. Years later, one teacher remembered that before Sheppard's arrival, he would be able to do a little teaching in the morning, but after lunch and recess, which were almost always out of control, he would rarely be able to focus students on academic work at all.

Initially Sheppard found it necessary to suspend a lot of students in order to establish control and clearly set expectations for students. But he also brought in the Responsive Classroom program, which helped develop a school-wide process and way of talking about discipline issues. Before long, students knew the rules as well as the teachers. If they were told to go to the principal's office, they would say things like, "But we haven't done step three yet," referring to the fact that when students got angry, they were expected to go sit in another teacher's room for a little while to calm down.

Sheppard also instituted structured recess where students would play specific games under adult supervision. After a while, recess was able to be a little less structured as children learned to play together without bullying and fighting. At the same time, Sheppard was helping teachers establish classroom routines like morning meetings and helping students manage disagreements without fighting. Signs in classrooms suggested phrases such as, "I see your point but have you considered . . ." Improved classroom instruction, with discussions of literature and historical events, gave students the opportunity to try out such phrases. With routines in place and better instruction, discipline issues at Dayton's Bluff died down to the normal issues faced by any school.

A recent report illuminates the importance of establishing the right disciplinary environment; it found that students' achievement was more strongly associated with school safety than neighborhood poverty, neighborhood crime, or the human and social resources in students' homes.[5] Even without the research, these principals know that unsafe and disorderly schools inhibit teaching and learning, so make sure to craft the right policies that everyone can abide by and allow teachers and students to focus on the activities of schooling.

Many It's Being Done leaders divide discipline issues into problems that should be handled by teachers—such as missing pencils and fidgetiness—and those that can't be handled by teachers alone.

So, for example, if a teacher at East Millsboro has tried all the usual procedures and is still having trouble with a child, she fills out a form and within a day or two a meeting is assembled of all the relevant people—parents or other family members, the counselor, the social worker, the principal, the teacher, and anyone else who might be helpful to think about what else needs to happen. Does the child need to see a counselor? Is there something going on in the family to the extent that a social worker's services are needed? Does the child need a mentor to meet with regularly? A plan is developed, and then a couple of weeks later the issue is revisited to see if the plan has helped or whether something else needs to happen.

By establishing clear processes that teachers can follow when they feel they need help with an individual child, teachers feel supported and the responsibility for students is shared. But as schools establish the overall culture of respect and improve instruction so that more students are actively engaged in their learning and have less time to fool around, teachers need to rely on those processes less. In any school there will be discipline issues, but these effective leaders report spending less and less time on discipline the longer they are there. "I spend hardly any time on discipline," Deb Gustafson of Ware Elementary said. "That doesn't mean we don't have issues, but I deal with them quickly and don't let them distract me from my main job."

Similarly, when Diane Scricca first arrived at Elmont Memorial High School, students frequently wandered the halls, either skipping classes entirely or arriving at class late and disrupting instruction. To address that kind of problem, high schools will often have "hall sweeps," and Scricca did the same thing. But she wanted the hall sweep to emphasize not just that students should be in class but that they had important work to do. So when the bell rang, all wandering students were sent to the auditorium where they were handed packets of work from the class they were missing and were required to complete it. Every professional in the building who wasn't teaching a class that period was involved in "sweeping" the students, handing them the packets, and supervising the work. "The first day we had 180 students. It was wild. The second day we had 18," Scricca said.

Again, they made an up-front investment to shift the culture and establish acceptable behavior. Spending the extra time and effort to have work for the students to do and to supervise that work paid off; once the routines and consequences were clear, Scricca and the rest of the administrative team no longer had to spend a great deal of time on the issue of wandering students. That means that administrators who in other schools spend all their time on discipline (a designated assistant principal, for example) were able to spend most of their time helping teachers improve instruction, which, not coincidentally, meant that fewer students were interested in skipping class.

The Elmont hall-sweep story emphasizes not just the focus on instruction but also the emphasis on all adults helping solve a problem. It's Being Done leaders take responsibility for every aspect of their building, but they are clear that there is no way they can do everything. They count on every adult in the building to play a role.

In terms of discipline policies, sometimes It's Being Done leaders are handed rules by their district, sometimes they consult faculty members about what rules should be in place. But if there is a rule, they expect every teacher and every staff member to enforce it. One day while walking through Elmont, John Capozzi passed a class that seemed deeply engaged in instruction, but he spotted something that disturbed him. "I hate that," he said. When he walked in the class, a student quietly slipped his hat off. Capozzi wasn't upset at the student—he knows adolescents will always test limits and that it doesn't pay to get angry at them. He was upset that the teacher had not enforced the rule against hats, thus undermining the school culture.

This same principle was illustrated by Ricardo Esparza who, after he left Granger High School, spent some time in a low performing Philadelphia high school as a visiting consultant. He stood in the hallway marveling at the fact that despite a ban on hats, hoods, and ear buds, hundreds of students went unchallenged by teachers, administrators, and the many security guards in the building. "The faculty voted on the rule," he said, "but only a few teachers enforce it. I don't know if *I* would have made that rule, but once it's a rule, everyone has to enforce it or the whole building feels out of control."

Discipline policies, in other words, are not just about enforcement by principals but about building routines and trust as well as creating teamwork among all the adults.

SCHOOL IMPROVEMENT PLANS

Another example of how principals leverage their administrative responsibilities into drivers for student achievement is the school improvement plan, which is a document many schools must produce to comply with district, state, or federal regulations. Many principals view school improvement plans as just another added task among many. Although they are supposed to be the product of "school improvement teams," many principals either write them in a last-minute frenzy or assign them to other staff members. Once completed, they are often forgotten about until the next year. What this means is that a great deal of time is spent on administrative compliance without actually being useful to anyone. Arelis Diaz said that before she became principal of North Godwin, the person who wrote the school improvement plan had intentionally put in "all kinds of silly phrases" knowing that the document would be filed away and no one would ever read it. "It would say something like, 'We will increase reading achievement by 10 percent in two years. The clown is on top of the moon.' It was so sad to me. It was a joke."

It's Being Done principals see the matter differently. They see the school improvement plan as a way to articulate a common vision and goals so that they and their staffs can hammer out concrete ways to address challenges, measure progress, and identify new goals. "We based everything on the improvement plan," said Natalie Elder of Hardy Elementary.

But they often have to contend, initially, with the more conventional view that the process is worthless. In fact, Diaz had difficulty recruiting anyone to sit on the school improvement team the first year she was principal. "They would say, 'That is such a waste of time,'" remembered Diaz. "I knew that in order to have success we needed to make the school improvement plan be an active document rather than just something we filed with the state and put away."

And so Diaz put the school improvement team at the center of the school's work. "I gave the teachers time to analyze what we were successful with—because we needed to celebrate—and where we were struggling," said Diaz.

So, for example, "We realized that in social studies, students really didn't understand the whole voting process and what elections meant," something that was tested in fourth grade on the state assessments. "Our fourth- and fifth-grade teachers felt this weight on their shoulders because they had the MEAP [state assessment]. And the kinder, first-, second-, and third-grade teachers felt very relieved that they weren't part of it. I gave the teachers time to break it down, and they broke it down to what kindergarten teachers were going to do, what first grade teachers were going to do, and so on."

In this way, the school improvement team began to act in ways that not only helped students do well on the state tests but actually aligned instruction across grades so that students were learning what they needed to.

Another example of how Diaz integrated the school improvement plan into the routines of the school was that she tied her classroom observations to it. Under the teacher contract in effect in North Godwin, teachers sign up for a particular time and lesson for formal observations. "I got so sick of seeing calendar lessons," Diaz said, describing a typical elementary lesson about the month, day, and year. After a few months, she told the teachers she only wanted to see lessons that addressed school improvement goals, and after a while she got even more specific. "I told them I didn't want to see any more lessons having to do with goals one and three but only two and four."

LEADERSHIP TEAMS

Throughout this book, we have talked about how It's Being Done principals empower staff to make decisions appropriate to their role to facilitate school operations and to relieve principals from lots of day-to-day administrative responsibilities. They do this with many instructional decisions as well. This is not something the principals can do immediately. They make an up-front investment in helping teachers make decisions and understand how to evaluate whether their decisions led to successful outcomes. They must establish shared core beliefs about students and how the school will run. In addition, they often need to help staff members feel capable of making decisions.

What this means in a practical sense is that the original leaders, who often needed to make substantial changes in culture, climate, and expectations, made many of the decisions early on in their tenure but gradually created routines to include more and more people in decision making. They never hand over responsibility, but they do share it.

When asked how decisions got made at Granger, Ricardo Esparza said: "Mostly school improvement teams (with my influence) and sometimes (rarely) I would issue a directive (with a good sell)."

In fact, 68 percent of the leaders report that leadership teams were the predominant model of decision making, with variation in how these teams were developed, who was included, and what they had influence over (see figure 5.2). For some decisions, whole staff input is sought.

As Mary Haynes-Smith of Bethune Elementary said, "I don't make any decisions without my team. I tell them what I see and ask what they think. A lot of times I've been wrong. Everything we do as a leadership team . . . Only in a life-and-death matter would I make a decision by myself, but it hasn't come to that."

At Centennial Place, Cynthia Kuhlman set up three committees with different responsibilities. "We had three leadership teams at Centennial with representation from each grade level and team (enrichment, etc.) on each leadership team. The grade-level team chairs met with the principal every Thursday morning at 7:30 a.m. to ensure good communication and logistics across the school. The grade/team chairs were responsible for communicating back to their teams and for bringing any concerns to the leadership team meeting. The Design Team was responsible for all matters related to curriculum and instruction and for leading collaborative planning activities. The School Improvement Council was responsible for all matters related to school climate and culture."

At Imperial High School, the leadership team identifies a problem or an idea they want to pursue, and they take it to the faculty senate for more discussion. The faculty senate consists of elected representatives from each of the departments, and each department gets one vote. "A recommendation from the faculty meeting is given, then a decision is made by administration with the faculty senate approval," said Lisa Tabarez.

Budgets are not considered a separate kind of decision—they are integral to how the school organizes itself for instruction and are treated as such.

Figure 5.2: Who makes decisions at It's Being Done schools?

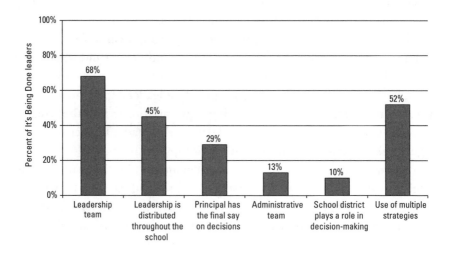

Note: n=31. Two principals did not provide responses.

Source: The Education Trust Principal Survey, Part 3.

So, for example, Barbara Adderley at Stanton Elementary helped faculty members understand how budget decisions should be made with a full understanding of student needs and then respected them enough to abide by their decisions:

We had an instructional leadership team where we met and discussed the issues of the budget. The union rep was part of that leadership team, and then I took their decisions back to the staff. Before we made any decisions that affected how we would move as a school, such as budget, I would put charts all over the library walls, and we did a gallery walk. So maybe one of the charts would talk about changes in curriculum resources, and the teachers would walk around and look at each one. We did something called Las Vegas voting where they would have colored stickers to vote on the most important things, and we would prioritize according to the voting. It wasn't just teachers in there—there were aides and others. But it all started with the data. Chrissy [Taylor] would share the math data; Kathleen [Shallow] would show us the reading data from Terra Nova and PSSA (the state tests). So if we wanted to order some interventions, we wouldn't order anything where the need wasn't indicated by the data. And the teachers made those decisions, and I had to accept those decisions. By the second year, when they looked at the data, they knew what they needed to do—because we had done the professional development.

Similarly, when Graham Road Elementary School's Title I budget was cut, Molly Bensinger-Lacy drew up a list of everything the federal money had been paying for and asked teacher leaders to vote on what to cut.

I always had a large leadership team that would advise me on issues and collaborate on writing the school improvement plan. However, during the first year, I made most decisions, with advice from a couple of outstanding teacher leaders and the assistant principal. Starting with my second year and increasingly with each of the following four years, a group of teacher leaders (what the DuFours might call a "guiding coalition") and I collaboratively made almost all decisions regarding hiring, professional development, deployment of resources including the budget, etc. These teacher leaders included team leaders, instructional coaches, reading teachers, and the math specialist.[6]

In other words, as her team developed expertise in decision making and in putting student achievement first, she gave over more responsibility and power to them.

A few principals (28%) talk more about listening to advice from faculty and staff but keeping the role as the final decider. "Some decisions I made alone, but I got input for many decisions," said Natalie Elder of Hardy Elementary. Teams are still evident here, but, on the surface, it appears to be less of a planned, inclusive, shared approach to decision making.

Diane Scricca is the exemplar of this approach and makes her point succinctly: "Benevolent despotism . . . always sought input from those who were focused on what was good for kids and had a strong knowledge of the issues . . . not a big believer in involving everyone just for the sake of collaboration . . . wasted precious time."

In all cases It's Being Done leaders—even when they keep decision making to themselves—make sure that the entire staff have ways to impart information and opinions so that they feel heard even when their views are not acted upon.

Although the principals work to create capacity for decision making in their school and rely more and more on leadership teams as practices and procedures are established, they are often in the situation of having to mediate between stakeholders with differing opinions on policies and how problems should be solved. For example, one group of teachers may want to institute a policy of automatic detention if a student fails to turn their homework in, while another group of teachers wants to institute afterschool tutoring. For most of these situations, an individual or group is apt to be unhappy with the decision of the principal. And although the principals felt that this is one of most difficult aspects of the job, they shared the same approach to making those decisions.

Ninety-one percent said that "the best interests of the students" guides their decisions in situations where faculty can't reach an agreement. Those who didn't specifically use the words "the best interest of students" reflected that it was important to understand the problem and what they had the capacity to do (see figure 5.3).

More often than not, they believed no explanations were needed about their decisions. Dana Lehman was crystal clear about what was important: "The decisions are always guided by student achievement—what will promote our mission best. The reality is that schools cannot be all things for all people. We are honest about that and about our priorities." Over time, the staff knows what to expect and respects that the principal is considering the bigger picture and what is best for everyone involved.

When asked how they communicated decisions, most of the principals had a transparent, "just explain it" type of approach. Those who didn't talk about explaining decisions to staff generally responded that they didn't need to explain the decision, as they were trusted and staff knew what to expect.

Cynthia Kuhlman went a little further with her response to express the importance of owning decisions: "One of my guiding principles was to internally make a commitment to our decision and to assume responsibility for it before communicating with stakeholders or staff. I never blamed

Figure 5.3: When faced with competing, legitimate priorites, how do It's Being Done principals make decisions?

Source: The Education Trust Principal Survey, Part 3, question 11, and www.wordle.net.

central office or the education department or whomever for my decisions. By the time I communicated to students, parents, or staff, it was my idea."

Sheri Shirley also captures the toughness associated with being the leader: "That's one of the hardest parts of my job. I'm just really honest. I lay everything out on the table. I have made decisions that have been very unpopular. I'm equally unpopular among all groups at times. I'm just really honest with my staff, but it's not really about me. Decisions just have to be made."

CONCLUSION

To be a principal is to have a difficult, complex job, and the high performing principals in our study show how to manage those multiple and often competing demands. They take on the responsibilities of running a school not just to comply with outside demands and ensure smooth operations with minimal conflict but wholeheartedly to meet the mission of student success. Where other principals might see a long list of chores, they see a few key leverage points: scheduling is about the strategic use of time; discipline is about educating students to be good citizens and creating a climate and culture conducive to teaching and learning; decision making is about building leadership throughout the building. It takes time to establish the right procedures and processes, but once they are established, they align with the mission of helping all students succeed academically.

CHAPTER SIX

The Really Tough Stuff
Creating a Climate and Culture

Of everything It's Being Done leaders do, creating the culture and climate is perhaps the most complex. Each school has its own unique way of operating that is dependent on its staff, district, and community and, like most institutions, is often resistant to change. Low performing urban high-poverty schools, in particular, are often demoralized places nearly incapable of the kind of collective decision making central to Its Being Done schools.[1] For school leaders to help schools—particularly dysfunctional schools—develop the capacity to change in order to meet common goals requires them to invest thought and time in their schools' culture and climate.

While we were struggling to come up with an adequate description of the culture and climate that characterize It's Being Done schools, we ran across the following quotation from Lt. Gen. Walter Ulmer, an expert on military leadership. He could have been writing about It's Being Done schools when he wrote:

> What is the essence of a "good climate" that promotes esprit and gives birth to "high performing units"? It is probably easier to feel or sense than to describe. It doesn't take long for most experienced people to take its measure. There is a pervasive sense of mission. There is a common agreement on what are the top priorities. There are clear standards. Competence is prized and appreciated. There is a willingness to share information. There is a sense of fair play. There is joy in teamwork. There are quick and convenient ways to attack nonsense and fix

aberrations in the system. There is a sure sense of rationality and trust. The key to the climate is leadership in general and senior leadership in particular.[2]

A teacher in an It's Being Done school, Laura Bailey, from Jack Britt High School, echoed much of what Ulmer said:

They'll say it's not about them, that "It's not about what I do as a principal, it's about what the teachers do in the classroom." But it all starts with our administration and our principal. They allow us to do our jobs in the classroom. They create the culture. They create the atmosphere of teamwork. If it weren't for that, our school would not be as successful as it is.

As crucial as this topic is, it isn't always easy to convince educators of its importance. When Deb Gustafson gives public presentations about what she and Jennie Black did to help Ware Elementary School improve, she says many school leaders dismiss the subject of culture and climate as "squishy." But she attributes a good part of the rise in Ware's definitely un-squishy test scores, particularly in the first year she was there, to improvements in culture and climate. As squishy and unquantifiable as it is, research documents that for both students and staff, connection to school is related to positive outcomes.[3]

Gustafson and Black were not alone in focusing on climate and culture in the first year. Thirty percent of the It's Being Done leaders said one of their initial goals for their school revolved around climate, culture, and relationships (see figure 6.1). In addition, those who came in to sustain the success of It's Being Done schools said one of their top priorities was to maintain the culture of the school.

The climate of a school is analogous to what we mean when we talk of climate in respect to weather, and describes in a general way what to expect. On any given day the weather may be atypical, but over a long period you pretty much know how much rain will fall and what the average temperature will be. Much of school climate has to do with things that really cannot change or can't change easily—the students, the parents, the building, and the available resources. But it also has to do with ongoing

Figure 6.1: What was your initial goal when you took over the principalship?

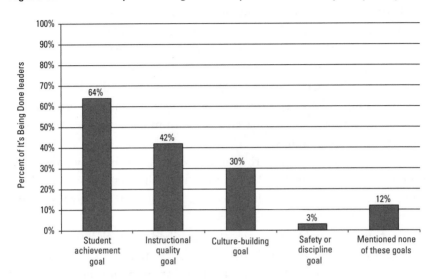

Source: The Education Trust Principal Survey, Part 3.

conditions created by the people in the building. A school can have a climate of respect or of disrespect, teamwork or isolation. Culture has to do with how the people in the school react to the climate and the daily weather conditions in the building. Do they band together to keep warm in a cold snap or hoard their firewood so that only some survive?

The key to both is, as Lt. Gen. Ulmer said, "leadership in general and senior leadership in particular."

IT BEGINS WITH RESPECT

It's Being Done leaders begin with an attitude of respect. At the most basic level, they respect the abilities of their students to succeed academically and to be productive citizens.

Respect forms the foundation for the relationships they have with students, but it also becomes part of their vision for the school, a vision they communicate through a number of different ways depending on their personal style.

In chapter 4, we talked about the ways It's Being Done leaders put their academic expectations into daily practice in their schools; they put their attitude of respect into their daily practice as well and help their staff do the same by explicitly making it a priority. They don't just tell teachers to be respectful but model speaking respectfully during interactions with students and teachers, provide tough but respectful feedback when there is a problem, and strategically use staff meeting time and professional development time to create shared ways of thinking, acting, and engaging with students and families.

In chapter 4, we also saw that all the leaders in this study considered themselves instructional leaders, but in this desire to reshape the culture and climate, they are also fitting what the academic literature calls "transformational leadership" as well.

Most It's Being Done principals described strategies they used to inspire and motivate their staffs, which was integral to the respectful culture they were actively attempting to create in their schools. Some of the particular strategies they used included telling stories of individuals and schools who beat the odds and how they did it, book studies on strategies they wanted to implement in their school, and sharing and celebrating their own school's data as evidence both that all children are capable of being successful and that they had the skills or could develop the skills to help them be successful.

So, for example, when Deb Gustafson first met with teachers at Ware Elementary, she told them she would never "write them up"—that is, document some failing in their personnel file—for anything except treating a student disrespectfully, by which she meant not just yelling but also speaking in a sarcastic or demeaning way. Some teachers protested at first, saying that they were simply responding to the disrespect shown them by the students, but Gustafson held firm that it is the grownups in a building who establish the climate. "How kids function is an absolute consequence of how adults function," she said.

To help teachers learn how to control their classes without sarcasm and humiliation, she and Jennie Black led book studies with the book *Teaching with Love and Logic: Taking Control of the Classroom*, by Jim Fay and David Funk, which gives concrete ways that teachers can handle students' misbehavior respectfully. In other words, instead of just insisting that teachers respect students and punishing their way to the goal, they created a process for the staff to work together to develop different ways of interacting with students that were in some ways quite different from what they were used to.

The issue of how It's Being Done leaders think about discipline is treated in more detail in chapter 5 because it is a key part of managing school buildings. For this chapter, the important point is to understand that It's Being Done leaders assume that every student wants to be successful but also understand that, as Diane Scricca of Elmont said, "Kids will always dig themselves into holes—because they're kids, and they're going to make mistakes. It's our job to throw them a rope so they can climb out." They are clear that students need to learn from their mistakes and suffer the logical consequences of their actions. No student can be allowed to interrupt the instruction of other students. But if students are having difficulties, that means the adults in the school need to examine their practices, think about what they could do differently, and work together with students to reengage them.

In fact, one of the things often said by It's Being Done leaders is that their goal is to treat every student the way they would like their own children to be treated. That leaves a lot of leeway for individual styles—some It's Being Done leaders are more casual, some more strict, and they respect this variety in their staff as well. They do not expect their staff to all behave the same way, but the underlying attitude must be based on respect for the abilities and aspirations of students.

This is another way of demonstrating high expectations for students, and when done with authority and authenticity, students respond and also invest the time and effort into meeting expectations.

It is hard to quantify exactly how important this is, but it automatically short-circuits some of the problems that plague many high-poverty and high-minority schools where low expectations are the norm for both students and their parents. When the adults in a school building believe that some students will not succeed academically or are—to put it at its most stark—headed to prison, they inevitably begin to sort students into those who are worthy of attention and those who are not. We have heard teachers say on the first day of school, "I can tell who is going to go to college." This perception about students, whether automatically or unintentionally, creates different sets of standards and expectations that are antithetical to It's Being Done schools' cultures.

One thing that happens in a school where not all students are expected to do well is that staff members often sort themselves out in terms of whether they agree with the general assessment of any one particular student or set of students. Some teachers prefer to work with those others think are less able. Think of the old sitcom *Welcome Back, Kotter*, where the teacher chose to teach students who with false bravado called themselves "sweat hogs" because they were the lowest academic track in the school. Some teachers prefer to spend their time and energies on those deemed the most able. Think of the teachers who clamor to teach honors classes, AP classes, and classes for students who have been identified as "gifted."

The inevitable result in such a school is a fractured sense of mission. There can't be a seamless working toward the same goal because there are different goals for different students and very different expectations for what different teachers do. Inevitably, resentments grow among teachers who are working toward different aims, and sometimes ugly things are said about how "those kids" don't deserve time and attention.

These are the kinds of schools that many of the original It's Being Done leaders took over, and many of them talk about having to build a common vision to replace the "toxic" environment into which they walked (see figure 6.2). "The staff believed that no matter what they did the students were too dumb to learn," said Sharon Brittingham about the context into which she walked at Frankford. Similarly, Barbara Adderley of Stanton said, "The culture was one of believing that children couldn't learn to high levels. These were the most vulnerable children in the community, and because there was no belief they could learn, the children had taken ownership of that. The principal was incompetent, and the teachers closed themselves in their rooms. There was a culture of believing that children couldn't control themselves, and that's the way it was and always would be, and teachers couldn't wait until three o'clock to go home."

As Adderley confirms, just as inevitable as the fractured sense of mission is the way students react to adult expectations at the school. When adults

Figure 6.2: It's Being Done principals create a common vision for their schools around achievement

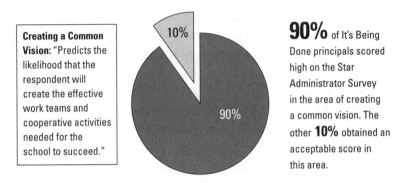

Creating a Common Vision: "Predicts the likelihood that the respondent will create the effective work teams and cooperative activities needed for the school to succeed."

10%

90%

90% of It's Being Done principals scored high on the Star Administrator Survey in the area of creating a common vision. The other **10%** obtained an acceptable score in this area.

Source: The Star Urban Administrator Questionnaire, Haberman Educational Foundation at the University of Wisconsin–Milwaukee, http://www.habermanfoundation.org/StarAdministratorQuestionnaire.aspx.

don't expect much of them academically, some students simply accept that assessment and think of themselves as low-achievers; some become angry; some react with a combination of the two. A few might defy expectations and succeed in the face of low expectations, but many more students simply disappear or hang around school only because that's where their friends are.

Differences in expectations of students can also exacerbate deep divisions and tensions among students themselves as they sort themselves into the "smart" and the "not smart" kids. Contrast that with what a senior at Imperial High School said: "At other schools, it's, 'There are the smart kids.' Here, we're all the smart kids."

Expectations flow into school-wide practices. For example, at University Park, all high school students take honors classes. With no multiple tracks, staff spend their time thinking about how they can ensure all kids meet that same standard. That doesn't mean, however, that it is an automatic process. Students who come in as behind as students do at University Park need a great deal of preparation for honors classes, preparation that begins in the summer before they begin seventh grade. But, says principal Ricci Hall, even if they can't read and write well when they arrive—and most can't—"they can still think." And so the seventh- and eighth-grade teachers immediately begin having the students grapple with important historical and literary problems even as they are working on decoding, fluency, grammar, and spelling.

In this way, faculty members demonstrate their respect for the abilities of students—while taking responsibility for teaching them what they need.

Students know and understand this difference. An African American senior at Elmont Memorial High School said, in recognition that as a young black male he is sometimes viewed outside school as potentially dangerous: "Some people may see you as a criminal, some people might see you as a great student. You have to see what the teachers see in you . . . The staff here really cares, they really try to get you to graduate. That's why I really like this school."

This is what Harvard researcher Ron Ferguson calls the "high support high demand" that all students respond to, which seems particularly important to African American students. University of Chicago scholar Charles Payne explains it this way:

> Whatever intellectual demands mean to everyone else, they mean something more to Black kids and other stigmatized populations because they are in dialogue with a different history. Demanding behavior, properly couched, welcomes you to the table; it signifies your membership in the larger moral and intellectual community. Like the rest of us, kids may enjoy an undemanding environment if they can get it; once they get accustomed to it, it can be a real project to change their habits. At the same time, they can be sophisticated enough to understand, at some level, that it means somebody thinks they can't do better.[4]

When Elmont Memorial High School eliminated the "modified" (or remedial) classes in which most of the African American students had been placed and expanded Advanced Placement course offerings; when University Park Campus High School offered only honors-level classes; when Imperial High School automatically enrolled students in college preparatory classes; and when Jack Britt assigned its best teachers to the most struggling students, all the schools put into practice their respect for student abilities and their expectations that they belonged in the "larger moral and intellectual community."

RESPECT EXTENDS TO FAMILIES

It's Being Done principals go even further, respecting their students' parents and assuming that all parents want their children to be successful and will do what they can, particularly if they are provided support and welcomed as important partners in the process. These leaders know that many of their parents aren't going to embrace the stereotype of involved parents attending PTA meetings and baking for the spring fair; some parents are working two and three jobs, and others are so disaffected that they feel uncomfortable in school buildings. And yet, these leaders say over and over, "They love their children."

This is an important point because in many schools teachers blame parents for students' academic failures. Melinda Young of Wells Elementary said that before the culture of respect and high expectations was established, "The parents blamed us, we blamed the parents. It was the blame game and we didn't get far."

In addition, parents who are not treated with respect—in particular, parents who see their children's abilities dismissed—often become frustrated, angry, and distrustful of educators, especially if they were not successful in school themselves.

A few It's Being Done principals have had to deal with the issue of parental anger, particularly in the early part of their tenure.

Barbara Adderley, for example, described the parents upon her arrival as "out of control." Von Sheppard said that many parents at Dayton's Bluff who felt their children had been mistreated had been accustomed to storming into the school and yelling at teachers. By locking classroom doors and insisting that parents speak with him first, he immediately helped teachers feel safer. But he didn't just close out parents. "I also gave them a vision of what I saw. I told them with all of the pain, bad press, and low teacher morale, that we were in a dark tunnel, but there was a light, and by the end of the year we were going to be walking out of this tunnel holding our students' hands and we were going to celebrate." It didn't take long, he said, before parents became partners in the process, because they understood that Sheppard was determined to help all students be successful.

In Mobile, Terri Tomlinson and Debbie Bolden found themselves as the focus of anger of many African American parents, steeped in distrust for generations, who were convinced that these two white women would not care about their children. Their consistently respectful treatment not only of students but everyone eventually won them the support of parents and community. The outward signs of this respect involved never raising their voices and always assuming that everyone acts from good motives, even when the actions themselves were unacceptable. Over time they found that going to parents' homes to meet with them demonstrated another kind of respect, because they were willing to meet parents on what Bolden called "their turf." Parents who were visibly uncomfortable and angry in the school building became welcoming hosts in their homes, Bolden said.

This is one example of how leaders challenged a barrier that was preventing the students and school from moving forward and changed existing practices and routines that established a respect between students, teachers, and families that otherwise would have gone unaddressed and left to fester, slowing the progress of improvement.

It should be said that It's Being Done leaders differ fairly widely in how much energy they put into bringing parents into the process. Molly Bensinger-Lacy of Graham Road is perhaps the extreme on one end of the spectrum. Although she would have liked to do more to reach out to parents, she felt her time and resources needed to be concentrated on the students in the building, and she limited herself to doing what she considered absolutely necessary—curriculum nights, awards nights, and other fairly standard forms of parent outreach. Barbara Adderley of Stanton went a bit further. Her parent liaison set up parenting classes, especially for her youngest parents, that included basic home economics concepts such as how to set up a food budget. Arelis Diaz of North Godwin established a whole program to bring parents in, teach them the curriculum, how to use computers, help with job searches, and volunteer in classrooms.

Ricardo Esparza, principal of Granger High School, is adamant that parents need to be "part of the equation." When he first arrived at Granger he arranged a door-knocking campaign by faculty members to students' homes. Armed with information about high school graduation requirements and more general civic information, such as election registration information, Esparza and faculty members invited parents to share their dreams for their children and helped them feel that school would work to make their dreams of graduation and college-going a reality.

That doesn't mean that Esparza ignored the many difficulties faced by their students' families. He and the other It's Being Done leaders know that many of their students' families are unable to provide the rich experiences that many middle-class families provide their children, and many don't know how to help with homework.

Some of the leaders bring parents together to help them learn what their students are learning and how to help their children be more successful. For example, Elain Thompson and Valarie Lewis held parent academies on Saturdays at P.S./M.S. 124 to teach parents while their children were involved in enrichment activities. "Some of them didn't know how to color with their children," said Lewis. "We taught them that skill." Other It's Being Done leader ask parents to read with their children, knowing that this can be a lot for families who are under great stress but respecting the parents enough to have expectations of them too.

In all these examples, the leaders intentionally try to short-circuit negative cycles of interaction by having respect—for students and parents— at the core of their approach. This is not out of a sense of pity but a sense that even students with tremendous disadvantages are able to become productive citizens and that even parents without many resources can become partners. They believe that it is up to educators to provide the experiences students need to excel. To this end they build routines and practices that demonstrate their respect every day.

By establishing the clear vision that every student will be academically successful and that it's up to the school to do what is necessary to achieve that success, It's Being Done leaders bypass the cauldron of dysfunction that can engulf schools characterized by low expectations of students.

This vision is not easy to create, but, as we saw in chapter 4, It's Being Done leaders intentionally produce this change in their schools.

RESPECT FOR TEACHERS AS PROFESSIONALS

This climate of respect doesn't stop with students and parents. It's Being Done leaders similarly respect the abilities of their staff members and demonstrate that respect through the same kind of "high support high demand" that they provide students—that is, they do not expect perfection but do expect teachers to think about how to improve and grow. Moreover, they don't expect them to do that alone but within a community of professionals.

Denise Garison, principal of Jack Britt High School, said that the most important factor contributing to the success of Jack Britt is "building a culture" of high expectations: "understanding what we as teachers must expect out of each child who comes through our doors. We must expect the best out of each teacher, custodian, administrator, bus driver, and every stakeholder of the school."

Similarly, Terri Tomlinson of George Hall Elementary said that she always listens to the ideas of teachers about how to solve problems, "because they're much smarter than I am." Her respect for teachers' expertise does not mean she ever lets go of her role as the person who sets performance standards, but she encourages teachers to try new things that they can demonstrate have a chance of working and which can be judged against some kind of performance data.

So, for example, when teachers at George Hall realized how limited the vocabulary and background knowledge was of their students, they began lobbying to take field trips. Tomlinson was initially wary, knowing from experience that field trips can suck up huge amounts of time, money, and effort with little payoff in the way of student learning. She allowed teachers to move ahead, but made sure that field trips could be justified by making sure that teachers did careful research, prepared students for the new sights and sounds they would experience, and thought deeply about the vocabulary and background that would be developed and nurtured. Today the school has an extensive field trip program in which every class goes on a trip almost every month. Students prepare ahead of time, video their experiences, write essays, and post blogs about them. Everyone in the building agrees that the field trips have helped their students become more successful by providing them more opportunities to interact with the larger world and building vocabulary and background knowledge.

This is an example of the way It's Being Done leaders demonstrate their respect for their teaching staffs without ever ceding their authority. They encourage their teachers to be creative to meet the needs of their students, but require that they provide a good basis for their actions and can demonstrate results. If the results don't work out as planned, these principals don't respond with recrimination—after all, not everything can work every time—but they do offer a reason to rethink and either recalibrate or start over again. After all, deep learning is often a matter of trial and error coupled with dispassionate evaluation.

The goal for student learning is shared, but working out the steps and processes to get there may be different for different teachers and different students and may change over time. As they want their teachers to know their students individually and plan accordingly for them, they try to do this with teachers. Their goal is to bring all teachers to the same high level of performance, but this requires different methods for different teachers and continual monitoring.

A part of that process is deeply discomfiting, because when people put time and energy into any new project, they want it to be successful. It is difficult to always be the person who says, "How can you demonstrate it was successful?" In playing that role, It's Being Done leaders often have to help teachers understand that, as Terri Tomlinson said in chapter 4, "It's not personal, it's business." To return to the opening quotation of this chapter, this is a way of providing "quick and convenient ways to attack nonsense and fix aberrations in the system." Helping teachers step back from their pet projects and cast their own gimlet eye on results is part of how It's Being Done leaders help "professionalize" their schools, within a climate of respect.

But as uncomfortable as that process is, another aspect can be deeply motivating for teachers, because it means that they are encouraged to keep developing new expertise, continually experiment with new ways to do things within the classroom, and share what they have learned with other teachers. To return once again to the opening quotation, "There are clear standards. Competence is prized and appreciated. There is a willingness to share information. There is a sense of fair play. There is joy in teamwork."

Or, to turn once more to Laura Bailey of Jack Britt High School, "We're not scared to mess up. If we mess up the [administrators] will have a discussion with us, but we're not scared."

BUILDING RESPECT THROUGH RELATIONSHIPS

It's Being Done leaders recognize that children must feel connected to their teachers in order to learn from them. As a result, these leaders are adamant that the teachers they hire understand the importance of relationships. At Jack Britt, one of the questions posed to potential hires is, "How important is it that students like you?" Denise Garison said that she doesn't want to hear the fairly standard response among many high school teachers that it isn't important whether the students like them as long as they respect them. "Students won't learn from someone they don't like," she said. She is, of course, exaggerating to make a point. Some students will learn from any teacher. But Garison is talking about the students she is most concerned about—students who enter behind and need to catch up. To do the hard work needed, they are going to need to have a friend in their intellectual corner, urging them to ignore past failures and convincing them that they are capable of doing the work necessary to succeed.

In describing a successful teacher, Molly Bensinger-Lacy echoed all It's Being leaders when she said: "A successful teacher is one who, in a caring classroom climate, brings all her students to grade-level benchmarks or beyond, thereby convincing each student that he/she is capable and desirous of high academic achievement. She also creates a sense of community so strong with and among her students that their resilience to triumph over all obstacles in their way of becoming contributing citizens is significantly increased."

It's Being Done leaders are clear that teachers are responsible for building powerful relationships, but each approaches the issue a little differently. Elementary schools can rely on the fact that teachers are with their students for extensive periods of time, providing many more opportunities to truly get to know the students, but secondary schools, with departmentalized classes, have to overcome the hurdle that each teacher is with students only for one subject for a limited amount of time.

Even at the elementary level, though, many It's Being Done leaders institutionalize practices across classrooms and teachers that support the development of relationships. So, for example, many of the schools have "morning meetings" where students and teachers talk freely about problems that have arisen and possible ways to solve them. Many also have mentoring programs where staff members, and sometimes outside volunteers, are enlisted to develop one-on-one relationships with students, with such activities as having lunch together, playing board games, and reading together. In this way they are building on the research literature on developing resilience in children, which has found that even children who live in very difficult circumstances have a good chance to be productive citizens if they have a strong relationship with just one adult who believes in them.[5]

At the secondary level, one way It's Being Done schools institutionalize the expectation that teachers will develop relationships with students is by requiring that teachers be in the hallways during class changes, greeting each student as they arrive in class and involve every student in classroom discussions. At Lockhart Junior High School, Susan Brooks went even further and required that teachers regularly document for her that every student in every class was asked a question every day. At first teachers found keeping track of this clunky and cumbersome (some used index cards, others checklists), but practice made this seamless. It ensured that, as Brooks said, shy, awkward, and quiet students couldn't just drift through junior high school with no one really noticing them, as happens too often in other schools.

Jack Britt has an extensive extracurricular program in which students and faculty members are able to spend time together in other activities outside the traditional classroom, but principal Denise Garison is convinced that the school's four-by-four schedule, which means that each student only takes four classes per semester for ninety-minute classes each day, also contributes to the school's sense of community. Teachers have only 80–100 students in a semester, in comparison to an ordinary high school teacher's 130–150 or so, allowing them to get to know and understand each student, their strengths and weaknesses, and what motivates them. However, highly successful Elmont has what could be considered the opposite schedule, with a nine-period day of forty-three-minute classes each. Elmont teachers are expected to build relationships with their students in class, but the school places a great deal of emphasis on the role of extracurricular activities in helping build a sense of community. When Diane Scricca first arrived at Elmont, she was horrified that most sports and clubs were overseen by people from outside the building. "I asked everyone I hired to take on one activity," she said. By the time she left, all teams and clubs were overseen by teachers from within Elmont.

Ricardo Esparza, a former wrestling coach, poses the problem with forming relationships as many high school teachers see it. "If I asked you to coach 140 students, you'd say that was impossible. That's what we ask high school teachers to do. But if I asked you to coach 15 or 18 students, you would say that's doable."

Acting on that assumption, Esparza broke up his student body at Granger High School into advisory periods where every certified professional in the building—the librarian, the counselor, and all the teachers—had a "case load" of between fifteen and eighteen students they mentored. The advisory periods met four times a week, during which they worked through a curriculum provided by the State of Washington that focused on all kinds of topics from balancing a checkbook to how to apply for college. These are topics that many high school teachers express frustration that there is little or no time to teach—topics that could help students be more successful in life but that don't fit into a standard academic schedule. Students at Granger met with the same mentor all four years. In addition to helping students master the curriculum, it was the job of the mentor to keep tabs on the academic work of their students and to meet with their students' parents or guardians twice a year to ensure that everyone—students, parents, and school—all understood where the student stood.

Esparza started this process early in his principalship after an encounter with a parent who was devastated that her son wasn't going to graduate even though he had gone to school every day. She hadn't realized that he had earned so few credits in his four years that he only qualified as a sophomore. "I didn't want that to ever happen again," Esparza said. So he required that each mentor meet with every student's parent or guardian once a semester. The meetings were actually run by the students, who followed a standard protocol where they reported on their reading level, credits accumulated, credits still needed to graduate, and grades up to that point. The teacher was responsible for ensuring that any of their colleagues' concerns were expressed—perhaps the student hadn't been attending class or turning in homework. The teacher would then commit the school to whatever had been agreed upon. Perhaps the math teacher had offered some afterschool tutoring, or the English teacher had offered to go over an essay during lunch. The student then said what he or she would do in the future (perhaps commit to reading a certain number of books), and the family committed to whatever they could do to support their student— provide a quiet place in the evening for homework, for example.

In this concrete way Esparza established his vision that students, parents, and teachers all had a role to play in student achievement. He made sure they physically got together to talk about what it would take for students to learn more and graduate, what parents would do, and what the school would do, and in the process they at least began the process of building a relationship built on a common goal.

Before Esparza arrived, "back-to-school nights" at Granger had been very traditional, where parents went from class to class to meet with their children's teachers for a few minutes each. The first year Esparza instituted the advisory periods with mentors meeting individually with parents, 30 percent of the families participated. "The teachers wanted to celebrate because only 10 percent had attended the back-to-school nights," Esparza said. "I said, okay, we can celebrate, but we need 100 percent." The next year Granger had 60 percent, and for the following eight years there was 100 percent family participation in the meetings. It became part of the culture, and students quickly disabused any new students of the notion that they didn't have to participate.

That's not to say that there wasn't some sweat involved in getting 100 percent participation. Esparza many times had to ask teachers how they were doing in meeting their goal and to produce the documentation for their meetings. Even Esparza had to work at meeting the goal—badgering the students he was mentoring, calling families multiple times, and even meeting with families at their homes. But, as Esparza said, because it was a manageable number of students, no one teacher had an overwhelming burden.

Many high schools in the country have advisory periods, so they could do something along these lines, but because no important intellectual work is done in them and there are few expectations for their performance, they often turn into badly behaved homework sessions hated by students and teachers alike. Instead, at Granger, they were opportunities for relationship building and also opportunities to help students learn and follow through on the behavioral expectations of school (e.g., being prepared for class, doing homework, planning and time management).

Esparza's system had the added benefit of helping families understand the system of school and thus develop a deeper relationship with the school. Many of his students' parents and family members had limited education—in fact, 75 percent of Granger's graduates were the first person in their families to graduate from high school—and so often didn't understand the significance of grades and how high school credits worked. Through the twice-yearly meetings they could learn enough to monitor their students and be part of the educational process with their student and the teachers.

This example demonstrates how a leader sets a vision, makes it concrete through practice, monitors it, and doesn't let go because of difficulties but continues to monitor, encourage, and sometimes hector on the way to the goal. It's Being Done leaders may use different methods based on the unique context of their school, but the goals of establishing respect through relationships remains the same.

There is an additional point to be made about this, however. These are not relationships for the sake of relationships. "We don't need missionaries to go feel bad for poor kids," said Natalie Elder, who led Hardy Elementary School to make the most progress of any school in Tennessee. "We need teachers. We need to understand that the pathway out of poverty is education."

In other words, teachers need to have deep relationships with their students, but it is not simply to demonstrate caring. Molly Bensinger-Lacy of Graham Road says that when she arrived, the teachers cared about the students but were focused on meeting immediate physical needs like raising money to pay for electric bills or buying winter coats. It's Being Done leaders are working to develop the kinds of deep relationships that build trust so that students will learn more.

Similarly, It's Being Done principals understand that in order to trust each other enough to work together, teachers need to have deep professional relationships. They work to ensure that teachers get the opportunity to do so, mostly through the collaborative structures that were discussed in chapter 4. But they sometimes go even further, having book groups, retreats, and team-building activities that involve the entire staff.

One example comes from North Godwin where, Arelis Diaz said, many staff members "didn't even know each other's names" when she became principal, and the teachers' lounge was dominated by a "vicious, negative attitude" where teachers regularly complained about students, parents, and the administration. Diaz had been inspired by the "FISH! Philosophy," which, building on a widely circulated video of workers at a Seattle fish market having fun by tossing fish around while serving customers, argues that workplaces that embrace play and having fun can be much more productive and successful.

In addition, Diaz wanted to acknowledge that working in a high-needs school is difficult and can be very draining. "The work is hard, particularly in schools with a lot of at-risk children. It is physically tiring and difficult." Difficult work coupled with low performance—which is the position of many high-needs schools—can lead to demoralization. "When you have a poor attitude about everything, you don't even want to invest in the hard work" needed to change, Diaz said. Engaging staff members in playfulness would, she thought, show appreciation and counter demoralization.

To put that idea into action, Diaz divided the staff into four groups. Knowing that if the process weren't transparent she would be subject to criticisms on how the groups were formed, she put all staff members' names into strict alphabetical order and then counted off one through four. Not just teachers but the custodians, cafeteria workers, and bus

Figure 6.3: It's Being Done principals advocate for the needs of their students over the needs of staff

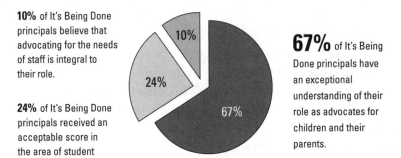

10% of It's Being Done principals believe that advocating for the needs of staff is integral to their role.

24% of It's Being Done principals received an acceptable score in the area of student advocacy.

67% of It's Being Done principals have an exceptional understanding of their role as advocates for children and their parents.

Note: Twenty-one It's Being Done leaders participated in the Haberman Star Administrator Survey. Leaders received a score of high, acceptable, or low along 13 dichotomous dimensions of leadership. These results represent the leaders' scores across the dimension of client advocacy. Principals who score high in this category tend to advocate for the needs of students, their parents, and the broader community, whereas principals who score low tend to advocate for the needs of staff. Due to rounding, these percentages sum to 101%.

Source: The Star Urban Administrator Questionnaire, Haberman Educational Foundation at the University of Wisconsin–Milwaukee, http://www.habermanfoundation.org/StarAdministratorQuestionnaire.aspx.

drivers were included. "Because it takes a village to change a school," Diaz said. She then tasked each of the groups to create "something playful" for the entire staff. One group created a spa in the teacher lounge with massages, soft music, and tea. Another created a cookie bar where everyone made cookies. "They were able to connect with each other and have a better attitude," Diaz said.

It's Being Done leaders invest time in developing direct relationships with their teachers as well. With family illnesses, marriages, and divorces, said Valarie Lewis of P.S./M.S. 124 in Queens, "The teachers come in with the same issues children come in with, but my job is to figure out what I need to do to support the teachers."

It's Being Done leaders often develop very close relationships with their staff. But as close as they are, It's Being Done leaders are clear that their primary covenant is always with students (see figure 6.3). In any conflict between what teachers need and what students need, students win out. "I wouldn't hesitate to have a tough conversation," said Terri Tomlinson of her staff at George Hall.

Keeping students at the center of school relationships can occasionally cause strain, but Molly Bensinger-Lacy of Graham Road argues that principals need to be honest with their teachers that what is best for students often means more work for teachers and that that kind of honesty is part of a respectful culture.

CONCLUSION

All It's Being Done leaders know that their commitment to students requires that they build a climate and culture that supports and requires excellence. They do this in part by respecting students as learners who are worthy of high support and high demand—that is, they expect them to work toward excellence in all their work. But they also respect teachers as professionals who are worthy of high support and high demand—that is, they expect them to work toward excellence in all their work as well. But they don't just leave it at expectations. They build in systems to monitor how teachers and students are doing and provide the support they need to reach their goals of excellence. To return where we began, with Lt. Gen. Walter Ulmer, they establish:

> . . . a pervasive sense of mission with a common agreement on what are the top priorities and clear standards. They prize and appreciate competence, share information, have a sense of fair play and joy in teamwork, establish quick and convenient ways to fix aberrations in the system, and establish an atmosphere of rationality and trust.

CHAPTER SEVEN

The Other Really Tough Stuff
Managing Outside Relationships

In previous chapters, we focused on the work principals do in their school buildings to improve teaching and learning. But principals operate in the larger world as well. Their schools are embedded in a larger system of education and are responsible to and part of school districts. Even Roxbury Preparatory Charter School has joined Uncommon Schools, a charter management organization, and thus will become part of a regional network of schools responsible to one another.

In addition, as representatives of community institutions, principals build relationships with outside constituents and organizations. The need to build relationships can be a burden but also represents a resource for the schools and their students. And the ISLLC professional standards for principals actually call on them to influence local, district, state, and national policy decisions affecting student learning (see chapter 2).[1]

In this chapter, we discuss how the It's Being Done leaders responded to these external responsibilities. As their schools are situated in very different contexts with different needs and levels of resources, the choices of the principals vary. However, all the leaders recognize and respect that they are part of a system and that public schools belong to the public and contribute to the public good. As discussed in chapter 3, these school leaders know that if their students don't get a good education, they most likely will face a life of limitations and dependence, which is not good for the students, but is also not good for the community.

This chapter is shorter than the rest, but it does not mean that this work is any less important or essential to the success of schools. Rather, it reflects our focus in this book on the role the It's Being Done principals play within their schools.

CENTRAL OFFICE: BEST FRIEND OR BARRIER?

Most of the It's Being Done schools are part of large districts with more than twenty schools (52%). Sixty percent of those large districts have more than one hundred schools, which means that many of the principals must manage rather complex relationships with their central office. Beyond variation in the number of schools, districts vary widely in their approach to managing and supporting schools, depending not only on the way their superintendents approach improvement but also by district characteristics (e.g., size, location, effectiveness, etc.) and existing state and local policies (e.g., decentralization and site-based management or standards-based reform and accountability systems).

Many It's Being Done principals argue that better systems of support for schools and principals would make the job easier and therefore more attractive to qualified people, which points to the fact that although some of the principals have strong working relationships with their central offices, others have quite strained relationships. Regardless of the tenor of the relationship, the principals generally think of the school as the "unit of change" and themselves as the leader of that change. By this, we mean that they believe the effective location of many decisions is at the school level where the expertise lies and where local contexts can be taken into account. As such, they view their districts as helpful when they support the needs identified by school staff and as unhelpful when they attempt to impose their authority and ideas on school processes without an understanding of the school context.

This is not to suggest that good, healthy relationships are that simple. Much like principals, the role and responsibility of districts has changed over time. As accountability systems have developed, districts are now being asked to take an active role in interpreting and mediating school response to state policy, including implementing curricular standards, graduation requirements, and school improvement plans. The ability or lack thereof of districts to take on these challenges might partly contribute to the rather common tension that exists between schools and the central office. The It's Being Done principals are thinking strategically about their own schools and want their district offices to think more strategically as well, differentiating among schools according to need, instead of managing with a simple compliance mentality.

For example, Arelis Diaz, who eventually became assistant superintendent of her district, said that when she was a principal, "I expected autonomy from central office. Instructional leadership is what creates results, not a manager. Managers can be puppets that do whatever central office says." She goes on to say that she had been willing to hand in her keys and go back to teaching if the level of autonomy and responsibility that she received was unsatisfactory. In her case it worked; the district is small with six schools, and she was getting results that no one had previously accomplished at her school. Thus, no one wanted to remove her from her school. But this isn't always the way it goes.

Generally, the It's Being Done principals would like autonomy. In addition to autonomy about instructional decisions, as in the above example, the principals also frequently mentioned wanting "true" autonomy over hiring and firing staff. Ricci Hall stated, "We also need more flexibility around hiring and ensuring that the right people teach in our classrooms." Furthermore, he says, "Districts need to provide opportunities for schools to be truly innovative and leave them alone when things are working."

In other words, our principals do not want to be told what to do, particularly when the data provide clear evidence that they are already on the right track. This desire for decision-making authority is not capricious. It's Being Done principals are willing to hold themselves and their staffs accountable for the results of their choices. They do not point fingers and blame external circumstances, but look inward and reflect on what they can do to achieve the goals they have set.

District Initiatives

In general, It's Being Done principals support high-quality proposals that lead to curricular coherence across districts — in part because many of their students move a great deal and would benefit from having a consistent, coherent curriculum in every school they attend. They are also invested in systemic change that will ensure more students receive a good education. Thus, they rarely object to district-wide initiatives around common standards and data-gathering. However, those are not the only kind of district initiatives they are asked to implement. Just as teachers around the country are subjected to the fads that get espoused at principal conferences, so too are principals subjected to fads that race through superintendent conferences. That, in fact, leads to one of the greatest challenges our principals face: what to do when they are expected to implement a district initiative that will disrupt what they believe is working.

The various responses from the It's Being Done principals in regard to a potentially contradictory initiative they are asked to implement by their district capture the tension and different experiences of the It's Being Done principals:

"This is the part of the job that is most challenging to me. These situations [getting a directive from central office that conflicts with school practice] make me feel like a middle manager rather than a leader because I don't set the vision. Central offices are there to support the schools, but they come up with ideas sometimes that come from other directives. The principal has to manipulate or buffer these probes from central office if they are going to negatively impact the school. You implement them, but you soften them and execute them halfheartedly."

"I don't comply, if it doesn't make sense . . . better to ask forgiveness than permission."

"I have always been the kind of leader that will back up my teachers when they say they need something, but when I get a directive from the district, I have to implement it regardless. I tell my staff that I understand them, but we have to try it. When I say this, my staff will try to give it their best shot. If it's not working, I'll tell central office. I'll give them my data, and the district usually lets me have some flexibility."

"We are a pretty small district, so it's pretty easy to talk openly with the district. Typically, the three elementary schools try to implement directives the same. Together, we usually try to find a way to make it work.

Sometimes, the district's hands are tied because they are getting directives from the state."

"We were so innovative they [Central Office] began copying what we were doing. They even made our school a demonstration site for others to learn from."

Underlying the varied experiences is a consistent theme. The principals know and respect they are part of a larger system. They know they won't have a job and can't help kids and teachers if they do not participate in the process. However, they do not cede their expertise and knowledge of their own school in the process. This goes for district initiatives as well as ideas they put forth and seek approval for from the district. For example, Sharon Brittingham felt strongly that all-day kindergarten was necessary for the students in her school. More than three-quarters of her students received free or reduced-price lunch, and nearly one-third were English language learners. When the board did not approve all-day kindergarten, she decided to use her Title I revenues to fund it. As she said, "I stood up for what I believed was right for kids."

Not only do they stand up for what they believe is right, they also think creatively to solve problems that arise due to the choices they make on behalf of their students. One principal in our study tells about the time she opposed implementing a new math program that she was convinced would not help her students as much as the one already in her school. She applied for a waiver and was allowed to use her existing program. However, she then had to figure out how she would pay for the materials her school needed—materials the district would not provide. Her solution: she took the district-provided materials for the new program, sold them, and used the money to purchase the materials she really needed.

Districts aren't always willing to grant such waivers. In those cases, these principals still feel that it is their responsibility to be the instructional leader for their school, and they are willing to invest the time, energy, and thought into how they can make new initiatives work with their current program. Jennie Black, at Ware Elementary School, reflected: "Sometimes it isn't always the way the district had initially planned, but we made it work for our school." Dolores Cisneros-Emerson agreed: "My philosophy is there are fifty ways to skin a cat, and I have found at least thirty-five ways so far." This was a common refrain from the It's Being Done principals; they tweak, adapt, make hybrids, and implement with an analytical eye, as Lisa Tabarez said. They have a plan for their schools and will not simply accept resources without spending the time to tailor them to the direction they are leading their school. These leaders make sure that what they bring into their school will cohere and align with what they are already doing. This is very different from some principals, who simply take direction or gobble up resources without attention to alignment and contextualization.

One principal, for example, told of how, after years of successfully using one particular reading program, the district decided to implement a new reading program. Both she and the teachers were dismayed—their students had been very successful with the old program, even if not all of the rest of the district's students had been. But she led the teachers through a careful study of what elements of the old program had been successful and which ones were actually part of the new program. When they realized that only a few things were left out of the new program, they worked out a way to incorporate in those elements and found that their students continued to be successful.

As Conrad Lopes said, "It isn't about programs, it's about people." These principals are not looking for silver bullets. Instead, they believe in creating professionals in their schools who rely on their expertise and that of their colleagues to guide their decision making. A few of the principals even went so far as to say they liked the challenge of being asked to use new resources. They believe education is about continually improving and apply that to themselves as well as the students. So, Denise Garison, principal of Jack Britt High School, said they try to be positive and are willing to consider that the program may be better than what they are doing or that parts of it could be utilized to improve their existing program. Most of all, they don't dwell on things. As Tom Graham said, they focus on getting the job done with students whether that is their first choice or they have to go to Plan B to comply with the district.

Support and Professional Development

Being a school principal can be a lonely job. There is no built-in peer group within the school, unlike for teachers. And because the It's Being Done principals feel their primary responsibility is to students, they put constant pressure on their staffs to improve, often asking them to teach and work in ways they have not been trained to do. It is not that they are not supportive and part of the team, but when someone has to be the heavy, that is their job. This means that they have few people within the school with whom they can share their dilemmas, which partly explains the close partnerships many make with their assistant principals and, when they can, with their predecessors. The close, ongoing relationship John Capozzi has with Diane Scricca, Ricci Hall with June Eressy, Valarie Lewis with Elain Thompson, and Denise Garison with Conrad Lopes all speak to the need professionals have to bounce ideas off people who fully understand the context within which they work.

Melinda Young has one of the more supportive districts among the It's Being Done principals, Steubenville City Schools. She and the elementary principals have a collaborative work group that enhances her work and gives her the opportunity to brainstorm with peers and work through issues. Similarly, Sheri Shirley said, "I have a great team of administrators in my district, and we do a lot of problem-solving together and sharing ideas." Like the other It's Being Done principals, she welcomes the opportunity to reflect on her practice. They do this with their own staff but appreciate an objective eye from outside the school to challenge them and help them think anew about their practices. Natalie Elder was part of a deliberate strategy by her district in Tennessee to build a principal cohort by regularly bringing in principals and assistant principals from similar schools to share training and solve problems together. Elder found the opportunity to think together with peers enormously helpful in sharpening her thinking and her strategies.

Cynthia Kuhlman mentioned how helpful she found quality staff-development opportunities provided by the Atlanta Public School District. Principals are busy people, but they want to keep up with new trends and strategies and appreciate having those opportunities made available to them by their districts. Too many of the principals, though, did not have these opportunities in their districts.

The previous discussion suggests that school districts are probably neither friends nor foes but that they often don't provide the kind of support principals need. Perhaps what we have learned from the It's Being Done Principals is that a better system of both structure and supports needs to be developed. These are all extremely competent leaders with core beliefs about their role and responsibilities that guide their decision making. Providing them with autonomy and flexibility is likely a wise decision, and they appreciate not being micromanaged. However, full autonomy could be a disaster for less prepared or competent principals. As Valarie Lewis reflected on her experience in New York City, she said, "There is a positive structure in New York City that gives schools their independence and lets me filter out the mandates. This works for strong leaders, but it's a recipe for failure for leaders that don't have direction." In other words, autonomy works for her, but its additional administrative burdens might topple less seasoned principals.

COMMUNITY CONNECTIONS AND RESOURCES

It's Being Done schools are located in all different types of neighborhoods and communities, from rurally isolated locations to Boston, New York City, and everything in between. As such, there are very different opportunities to exploit, but It's Being Done principals attempt to make use of whatever will help their students. Sometimes this means arranging for exposure to new environments, arts, and culture that students would otherwise not know of, but other times it means building collaborations with social or health service agencies to ensure the students' most basic needs are met.

And so, in regard to meeting the basic needs of the students, relationships with the community took a myriad of forms and purposes. For example, at Wells Elementary School in Steubenville, Ohio, the principal encouraged the school nurse to contact local businesses to try to get donations for eyeglasses for their students; Valarie Lewis at P.S./M.S. 124 works with local social service agencies to provide the mental health counseling for her students who need it; Terri Tomlinson at George Hall works with families to keep up their Medicaid eligibility and then makes sure that students get to necessary doctor visits; Sharon Brittingham at Frankford Elementary School realized a nearby community was home to a lot of retired professionals and engaged them to come in weekly and read to students; Barbara Adderley at M. Hall Stanton Elementary in Philadelphia worked with the Philadelphia Eagles to bring their mobile eye clinic for vision exams and eyeglasses.

One of the more comprehensive community relationships among this set of schools is that of University Park Campus School (UPCS), which was founded because of a partnership between Clark University and Worcester Public Schools. The educational program at UPCS is deliberately planned to help students prepare for college, and being located near the college campus gives students a vision of what college life is like. Students also get to take college classes to experience demanding academic courses that small UPCS can't offer to its students. Other, more indirect, benefits accrue to students through professional development of teachers by the clinical training program at Clark.

Centennial Place Elementary School didn't have that kind of relationship, but it exploited its location near Georgia Tech to bring special arts and science programs to the school. Students got to meet artists and musicians visiting the campus that they wouldn't otherwise have been able to accomplish on their own. For example, the students got to meet famous cellist Yo-Yo Ma, who enlisted them to help him evaluate the acoustics of the hall he was to play in.

In addition, many of the principals seek out grants and opportunities to both meet program needs and to provide "extras" to students, from additional computers and books to field trips and arts programs. They look for grants both small and large. Ricardo Esparza, for example, applied for a small local grant to be able to purchase additional books for the school library. Centennial Place had a "science in the arts" grant that let children learn, for example, about the physics of sound through music. The point is that they all use the resources they have available to help their students. They never allow outsiders to set the agenda, but if outsiders can help, they welcome them in. So, for example, Molly Bensinger-Lacy gladly worked with a business partner who wanted to provide backpacks and school supplies each year for every student but insisted that its generosity not be made into a media event that exploited students' privacy while promoting the business's image. But she did seek out and publicize a partnership with the Kennedy Center for the Performing Arts because that would expose her students to a world of art that would otherwise be foreign to them and that would give students a positive public image.

THE STATE AND NATIONAL POLICY CONTEXT

It's Being Done principals are bottom-line folks. They set goals and measure their progress toward those goals. Standards-based reforms and accountability systems don't scare them; in fact, these reforms provide the tools to assess how they are doing and the leverage they often need to make change. Not all agree that the standards in their state are high enough or rigorous enough to provide sufficient direction and leverage, and many see pieces of their state accountability systems as flawed. But most agree that standards and rigorous assessments are necessary and are tools that can be used for improvement and evaluation, when done fairly. In fact, they use all kinds of assessment data to monitor and track teaching, learning, and implementation of plans and programs in their schools. They understand that the pressure that comes from accountability—both inside and outside of their schools—provides some of the pressure in the support-pressure balance they know is necessary for a school to be high-functioning.

They would, however, like legislators to have a better understanding of what schools and the work is really like. Frequently changing mandates and conflicting reporting rules are a real source of frustration, as are unreasonable timelines and poor communication.

When asked about what they would tell or ask from legislatures, most say they would like more money. This is not greed or complaining, but rather comes from their desire to educate children and their knowledge about just how difficult that work is. One consistent theme about where they would like to spend additional monies: extended day and year schedules and extra supports for students, such as tutors. As Jennie Black said, "There is not enough time to get students to learn *all* they need to know."

That said, these principals aren't generally getting into policy debates and attempting to influence national decisions that affect student learning. They are working hard every day to do their jobs, in their schools and districts. They do, however, feel a powerful commitment to the field and to helping grow other leaders and sustain leadership in their schools. As Deb Gustafson said, "As school leaders, we must take responsibility for the next round of leaders for our schools. We must find the time to work . . . to prepare tomorrow's leaders. School leaders matter."

CONCLUSION

The ways It's Being Done principals handle external relationships are guided by their core beliefs about education and their passion to do whatever it takes to make sure students learn. This ranges from making sure all district programs and directives work for their students to finding community partners who can provide additional services, opportunities, and experiences that their students wouldn't otherwise have, and also growing their own skills through quality professional development and peer networks.

CONCLUSION

Not Superman

A New Kind of School Leader

In any field the difference between excellence and mediocrity often lies in the hundreds of decisions made by experts. Musicians weigh subtle variations in tone and timbre barely discernible to the uneducated ear that profoundly change their music; cinematographers manipulate minute differences in light that fundamentally alter the mood and complexion of a film; scientists control hundreds of variables in order to be able to make a conclusion about one. To those not steeped in the field, these experts' decisions seem to be based on a bewildering set of factors; for experts, they are the everyday stuff of life.

The thirty-three school leaders in this study whom we call It's Being Done principals work at a high level of expertise, weighing factors that nonexperts may not even realize exist but that often make the difference between successful schools and mediocre ones.

There is something else they share that is a little hard to define but is enormously important, and that is a democratic persona of the small d variety. These are not baseball-wielding law-and-order principals barking orders like Joe Clark, made famous by the movie *Lean on Me*. They approach the students, teachers, parents, and staff in their buildings with the kind of open, frank, and respectful attitude that the founders of the United States of America envisioned as the way free citizens should treat one another. They are hopeful without being unrealistic; hardnosed without being mean-spirited. They are all nice people—but with a character of iron—who expect everyone around them to excel.

It seems obvious that if we want better schools, we should understand what expert educators consider important. These are the people who are doing what we as a nation have asked them to do; their schools point the way to how we can help all our children read, write, compute, think, and prepare to be productive members of a democratic society. They have mastered complexities that elude much of the field.

None of which is to say that the It's Being Done principals in this study are perfect leaders running perfect schools. Each can—and does—point out deficiencies in the schools they lead. They know their schools' flaws, their teachers' shortcomings, and which of their students need more help. Similarly, they are clear-eyed about the mistakes they themselves have made. Terri Tomlinson of George Hall Elementary School, for example, has a daily discipline of reflecting on what went well and what she could have handled better.

But that's one of the points we hope this book makes—we don't need superheroes who never make mistakes. We need experts, and expertise can be developed and cultivated by educators with the honesty to discriminate between excellence and mediocrity, the courage to do things differently to improve, and the discipline to reflect on what factors lead to success and what can be learned from failure.

Unless we as a nation commit ourselves to recognizing and helping develop that kind of deep expertise among our school leaders, we will continue to be at the mercy of those who say that educating all children well is patently impossible or charlatans who peddle nostrums for our nation's education woes. We can't afford either—the stakes are too high; we are already falling behind other countries. As a nation we know we need better schools. What we need to understand is how to get them.

Earlier in this book we asked a set of five questions that research has posed about school leaders. We want to pose them again in light of what we have learned.

1. WHAT KIND OF SCHOOL LEADERS DO WE NEED?

Policy makers as well as researchers struggle with this question—do we need "transformational" leaders whose job is to change the culture and shake up long-established traditions and power structures? "Distributive leaders" who carefully share their powers among all the school's stakeholders? "Moral leaders" who lead courageous conversations? "Building managers" who keep schools safe so that teachers can teach and who make sure buses run on time so that students can get to school? Or do we need "instructional leaders" who are steeped in the craft of instruction and who can help develop expert teachers?

This question has deep implications for the kinds of people we try to attract to be school principals. If all we need are generic leadership and administrative skills, we can look to any field. Anyone who has successfully led a business, sports team, or military unit could be seen as a potential school leader.

So what kind of leaders are It's Being Done principals?

They say they are instructional leaders. They see their core responsibility as having to do with what children learn in their schools, and they draw deeply on their own instructional experience to, as Ricci Hall of University Park Campus School said, "create powerful learning experiences" for their teachers. Most were in classrooms for more than a decade—many with additional expertise in special education and English as a second language—and they have deep insight into the power that good instruction has for children who might otherwise be written off as incapable of learning to high levels. Even Von Sheppard, whose background was not as a classroom teacher, sees himself as an instructional leader. When he arrived at Dayton's Bluff, he straightforwardly told his teachers that he didn't know much about instruction. But because he was a coach and because he understood that instruction was the core business of a principal, he led his staff through a process of learning together about instruction.

So it seems that instructional leaders are the kind of leader schools need. And yet in listening to It's Being Done leaders talk about their practice, it seems obvious that at times they are also transformational and moral leaders in their willingness to change long-standing and comfortable routines and challenge those who would write off children because they come to school with little social capital. They are expert managers who ensure that building operations run smoothly and support instruction; that teachers get the supplies, feedback, and training they need; and that students get the teachers they need. And they all work to distribute leadership throughout their buildings because they know that schools are complicated organisms that need all the leadership they can get. "It's not my job to run the building," said Diane Scricca. "It's everyone's job."

In other words, even while instruction is at the core of what they do, their role cannot be limited by any one construct developed by researchers or politicians. It's Being Done leaders are the kinds of leaders their schools need, which means that they carefully assess their schools' strengths and weaknesses and then use their knowledge of instruction to develop the appropriate expertise among all the adults in the building and to create supportive structures around them. They use their core beliefs about the deep purpose of education and the capacity of all students to motivate their staffs and sustain their own courage and stamina in the face of obstacles.

Which leads to the second of our questions.

2. WHAT IS SCHOOL LEADERSHIP?

This may seem like an odd question in a way—shouldn't we know that by now? But as we noted in chapter 2, discussions of kinds of leadership, like the one above, sometimes focus on styles of leadership to the exclusion of the actual practice of school leaders, which to a large extent is about setting direction, developing people, and developing the organization.[1] If they do those things well, the rest of their school will be set up for success. Let's take these one at a time:

Setting Direction

It's Being Done leaders are uncompromising about the direction they have set and, despite big differences among the schools they lead, the vision is the same. They are determined that their schools will help all students be successful. It's Being Done leaders believe that they lead institutions that in many ways are the bedrock of our democratic society and thus have an obligation to prepare students to take on the responsibilities incumbent upon citizens of a complex democracy. To them, successful students are students who are confident, curious, love learning and reading, solve problems, know how to stand up for themselves, and understand their responsibilities to others. But these leaders also never lose sight of the fact that in order to have the opportunities that are available to educated people, their students need to master academic standards. By stating that as a clear goal, they provide an organizing principle which is consonant with developing good readers, writers, mathematicians, and thinking citizens.

To those outside schools it seems obvious that the goal of schools is to help all children master academic standards. After all, if that's not the goal of schools, then why require children to attend? But far too many people who work in schools think that's a utopian notion—particularly in schools where children arrive behind or their families don't understand how to support academic achievement.

It's Being Done leaders bring to the job a clear understanding that all children can learn to high levels and that it is up to them to set the performance standard and up to the schools, as Terri Tomlinson says, "to figure out the ways to teach them." And they are not satisfied unless students reach benchmarks that will put them on a pathway toward readiness for their future lives.

Developing People

Like the leader of any enterprise, It's Being Done principals think deeply about getting the "right people on the bus," in that oft-quoted phrase of Jim Collins from *Good to Great*. And for that reason they enthusiastically recruit teachers they believe can be excellent in their schools and unflinchingly work to rid their schools of those who they think harm their students. June Eressy, after leading University Park Campus School for many years, took the principalship of one of Massachusetts's lowest-performing schools in the 2010–11 school year. She told us that she encouraged one teacher to transfer at the end of her first year and added that he objected her assessment of him was personal. "It kind of is," she said she responded. "If you're not going to teach my kids, I take that personally."

But, she added, she sees her primary job as not simply hiring and firing but as developing teachers and helping them get better. Anybody can get good results from "stacking the deck," she said. She, like the other It's Being Done principals, know that the needs are too great to simply gather a district's best teachers in one or two schools to create islands of excellence; to improve all the schools, the expertise of everyone must be developed.

She and the other principals are well aware that there are deficiencies in the way we as a nation recruit, train, and induct teachers. They know that we have many teachers who don't have what Diane Scricca says is the "set of pedagogical skills to make a difference in their classrooms." But they also believe that, as Barbara Adderley says, "We can't hire and fire our way out of this." They believe that it is their job to build the competency and skill of teachers so that they, too, become experts and leaders.

Developing the Organization

It's Being Done leaders set up the kinds of processes, routines, and structures that mean that teachers and staff have the opportunity to reflect on what is going well and what is not and to plan on how to improve. They make sure that teachers have information essential to their work so that they can make instructional decisions on evidence not only from their classrooms but from other classrooms and schools. They work with teachers to develop content expertise and to share their expertise across their schools and—when they can—their districts. They also reach outside their schools to fill in gaps and expand the array of services necessary for their students.

In doing all this they are, in essence, developing a professional practice. Paul Reville, secretary of education in Massachusetts, once said that education is an "outdated vocation," not a profession. "We don't have any development program; we don't reward excellent performance; we don't have a career ladder; we don't have high-quality induction; we don't have supervision and evaluation. We just don't have the basic elements of a profession."

School by school, It's Being Done leaders are helping create those elements of a profession.

3. WHAT DO PRINCIPALS DO DAY TO DAY?

It's all very well to have a vision and set up systems, but they are no guarantee of success or excellence. Teachers around the country tell sad tales of all the high-falutin' plans by principals that never really got off the ground because no one followed through. That's why much of the daily work of It's Being Done principals has to do with what Valarie Lewis says is the need to "inspect what you expect." It's Being Done leaders are in data meetings making sure they focus on the instructional needs of individual students; they are in classrooms making sure teachers are able to establish respectful classroom routines and give their students high-level instruction; they are in alignment meetings making sure that teachers have an aligned curriculum across the grades; they are planning powerful professional-development opportunities for staff members who need help.

They are, in other words, holding everyone accountable for their jobs and helping those who need help to improve.

That may sound a bit scary, but Dannette Collins, a teacher at George Hall Elementary in Mobile, Alabama, says that what she most values about her principal, Terri Tomlinson, is that she "makes sure everyone does their work." In other schools where she has taught, Collins said, the principals didn't bother noticing whether teachers who agreed to take on a responsibility, such as developing materials for a commonly taught lesson, actually fulfilled it. She and other conscientious teachers were left feeling overwhelmed; not only did they have to do their own jobs, but they also had to pick up the slack of others who didn't—or risk harming students. This sense of being among the few people who actually do their jobs contributes to the burnout of good teachers, reinforces the model of private practice, and contributes to a fracturing of the school mission.

But exactly how do It's Being Done principals hold people accountable? Too often in U.S. schools, the only choice has seemed to be between zero accountability and a harsh, martinet-like system of control where people are told what to do and are punished if they don't follow orders, which doesn't build expertise or a culture or climate of respect. It's Being Done principals have developed a different approach that may lie at the heart of what distinguishes them from other, less successful principals.

They are, in a phrase, relentlessly respectful—and respectfully relentless.

Despite their distinctively individual styles, all these school leaders consciously attempt to model for their teachers and students the way free citizens should treat one another in a democracy—with tolerance, respect, and high expectations. They respect the abilities and aspirations of their students and staff members and assume that all want to be successful. But they are also relentless in efforts to ensure that students truly are successful. If teachers dismiss the abilities of students, they respectfully remind them that their job is to teach them and ask what their plans are to help those children meet standards. To a teacher whose class got out of control they might say, "Let's chalk that up to a bad day, but here are the things you should do tomorrow."

This also gets at something else they do every day, which is to manage the climate and culture of the building. They set the tone by always looking to learn from mistakes, not punish them, thereby creating a willingness on the part of students, teachers, and staff to learn new things. "We're never afraid to mess up," said one teacher in an It's Being Done school. "Our administrator will have a conversation with us, but we're not afraid." These principals work hard to create the right balance of pressure and support to ensure teachers grow.

4. HOW AND HOW MUCH DOES LEADERSHIP AFFECT STUDENT LEARNING?

Students learn from teachers, which makes teachers the most important contribution that schools can make to student learning. But that just raises the question of how teachers learn to work in the ways that help all their students learn. We know that inexperienced teachers report feeling unprepared when they first walk into a classroom; even experienced teachers often report feeling overwhelmed by expectations that they help all their students learn to high levels.

It is the role of school leaders to help organize the work; figure out how to shore up the knowledge and skills of teachers; establish a climate and culture that permits and requires high-quality work; and set up the routines and systems that ensure that what is agreed upon gets done.

We can't quantify the effect this has on student learning, but the results of It's Being Done schools are a powerful argument that it has a large effect. Certainly the principals in this study believe that their leadership makes a difference. If they didn't, many would probably return to the classroom, where they had found great professional satisfaction.

5. WHAT IS THE ROLE OF THE PRINCIPAL IN HIGH-POVERTY SCHOOLS?

The reason this seems such a compelling question to us is that high-poverty schools are one of our knottiest problems as a nation. All of the things that get in the way of children getting educated tend to happen more often and with greater intensity in high-poverty settings and schools.

Children who live in poverty often arrive behind in terms of vocabulary, background knowledge, and organizational wherewithal. Their parents are often unable to help their children overcome lackluster schools in the way many middle-class parents are able to do. The traditional school structure, marked by teacher isolation and autonomy, is simply incapable of responding to the many needs of children who live in poverty. Teachers in high-poverty schools can work hard and still fail, leading to a sense of futility and discouragement that permeates through classrooms and schools and sometimes leads to complete dysfunction.[2]

Such school dysfunction is not the fault of the children or their parents, but poverty and its correlates are often blamed, in part because it is easier to point to it than to reshape schools.

But in It's Being Done schools we can see that if the institution is reshaped in such a way that teachers are no longer lone cowboys but part of a highly efficient pit crew focused on the needs of individual children, all children will benefit.[3] And, even more important, students learn—many to very high levels that would be the envy of any middle-class school. When this begins to happen, teachers no longer feel overwhelmed but masterful because they see the success that eludes others in the field.

We are really just at the beginning of reshaping our schools to focus on the individual needs of children to learn, and it is high-poverty schools that have the opportunity to lead the way. If they can be successful—with the most vulnerable children in our society—by figuring out new ways to operate, this can lead the way for all our schools to be more successful than they are now.

It is at the school leadership level that this tough work of refashioning school structures must be done, which means that it is up to principals to establish the vision that all children can learn and then help everyone in their schools figure out how to help them do so.

Notes

2. So, What Do We Know About Principals and School Leadership?

1. Bradley Portin et al., *Making Sense of Leading Schools: A Study of the School Principalship*, funded by The Wallace Foundation, Center on Reinventing Public Education (Seattle, WA: University of Washington, 2003).

2. Scott Thomson, *Principals for Our Changing Schools: The Knowledge and Skill Base* (Fairfax, VA: National Policy Board for Educational Administration, 1993).

3. Lynn G. Beck and Joseph Murphy, *Understanding the Principalship: Metaphorical Themes 1920s–1990s* (New York: Teachers College Press, 1993).

4. Institute for Educational Leadership, "Leadership for Student Learning: Reinventing the Principalship," http://www.iel.org/programs/21st/reports/principal.pdf.

5. Philip Hallinger and Joseph F. Murphy, "Assessing the Instructional Leadership Behavior of Principals," *Elementary School Journal* 86, no. 2 (1985): 217–248.

6. Bernard M. Bass, *Leadership and Performance Beyond Expectations* (New York: Free Press, 1985).

7. Helen M. Marks and Susan M. Printy, "Principal Leadership and School Performance: An Integration of Transformational and Instructional Leadership," *Educational Administration Quarterly* 39, no. 3 (2003): 370–397.

8. Richard Elmore, "Building a New Structure for School Leadership," http://www.ashankerinst.org/education.html.

9. Kenneth Leithwood et al., "How Leadership Influences Student Learning," http://www.wallacefoundation.org.

10. Kenneth Leithwood and Carolyn Riehl, "What We Know about Successful School Leadership," http://www.cepa.gse.rutgers.edu/whatweknow.pdf.

11. Philip Hallinger and Ronald Heck, "Can Leadership Enhance School Effectiveness?" in *Educational Management: Redefining Theory, Policy and Practice*, ed. Tony Bush et al. (London: Paul Chapman/Sage, 2001); Jay A. Conger and Rabindra N. Kanungo, *Charismatic Leadership in Organizations* (Thousand Oaks, CA: Sage Publications, 1998).

12. Jim Collins and Jerry I. Porras, *Built to Last: Successful Habits of Visionary Companies* (New York: HarperCollins, 1997).

13. Scott Thomson, *Principals for Our Changing Schools: The Knowledge and Skill Base* (Fairfax, VA: National Policy Board for Educational Administration, 1993).

14. National Association of Elementary School Principals, "Leading Learning Communities: NAESP Standards for What Principals Should Know and Be Able to Do," http://www.naesp.org/resources/1/Pdfs/LLC2-ES.pdf.

15. National Association of Secondary School Principals, *Principal Professional Development* (Arlington, VA: National Association of Secondary School Principals, 2001).

16. National Policy Board for Educational Administration, *Educational Leadership Policy Standards: ISLLC 2008* (Washington, DC: Council of Chief State School Officers, 2008).

17. Martin Haberman and Vicky Dill, "Selecting STAR Principals Serving Children in Poverty," *Instructional Leader* 12, no. 1 (1999): 1–5, 11–12.

18. Harry Wolcott, *The Man in the Principal's Office: An Ethnography* (New York: Holt, Rinehart and Winston, 1973); Richard L. Andrews and Roger Soder, "Principal Leadership and Student Achievement," *Educational Leadership* 44, no. 6 (1987): 9–11; James P. Spillane, Eric M. Camburn, and Amber Stitzel Prega, "Taking a Distributed Perspective to the School Principal's Workday," *Leadership and Policy in Schools* 6, no. 1 (2007): 103–125.

19. Susanna Loeb, Eileen Horng, and Daniel Klasik, "Principal's Time Use and School Effectiveness," *American Journal of Education* 116, no. 4 (2010): 491–523.

20. Spillane, Camburn, and Prega, "Taking a Distributed Perspective."

21. Larry Cuban, *The Managerial Imperative and the Practice of Leadership in Schools* (Albany, NY: SUNY Press, 1988).

22. Bradley Portin et al., "Making Sense of Leading Schools: A Study of the School Principalship," Funded by The Wallace Foundation, Center on Reinventing Public Education (Seattle, WA: University of Washington, 2003).

23. James S. Coleman et al., *Equality of Educational Opportunity* (Washington, DC: U.S. Government Printing Office, 1966a).

24. Henry Williams, "Teachers' Perceptions of Principal Effectiveness in Selected Tennessee Secondary Schools," *Education* 121, no. 2 (2000): 264–276.

25. Ronald Edmonds, "Effective Schools for the Urban Poor," *Educational Leadership* 37, no. 1 (1979): 15–24.

26. I. I. Dow and W. F. Oakley, "School Effectiveness and Leadership," *Alberta Journal of Educational Leadership* 38, no. 1 (1992): 33–47.

27. Eric Hanushek, "The Economics of Schooling," *Journal of Economic Literature* 24, no. 3 (1986): 1141–1178.

28. Eberts and Stone, "Student Achievement in Public Schools"; Randall W. Eberts and Joe A. Stone Jr., "Student Achievement in Public Schools: Do Principals Make a Difference?" *Economics of Education Review* 7, no. 3 (1988): 291–299.

29. Dominic Brewer, "Principals and Student Outcomes: Evidence from U.S. High Schools," *Economics of Education Review* 12, no. 4 (1993): 281–292.

30. Philip Hallinger and Ronald Heck, "Reassessing the Principal's Role in School Effectiveness: A Review of Empirical Research, 1980–1995," *Education Administra-*

tion Quarterly 32, no. 1(1996): 5–44; Robert Marzano, Timothy Waters, and Brian McNulty, *School Leadership That Works: From Research to Results* (Alexandria, VA: Association for Supervision and Curriculum Development, 2005); Bob Witziers, Roel Bosker, and Meta Kruger, "Educational Leadership and Student Achievement: The Elusive Search for an Association," *Educational Administration Quarterly* 39, no. 3 (2003): 398–425.

31. Hallinger and Heck, "Reassessing the Principal's Role in School Effectiveness."

32. Karen Seashore Louis et al., "Investigating the Links to Improved Student Learning: Final Report of Research Findings," http://www.cehd.umn.edu/carei/Leadership/default.html.

33. Donald Boyd et al., "The Influence of School Administrators and Teacher Retention Decisions," http://www.urban.org/publications/1001287.html.

34. Marzano, Waters, and McNulty, *School Leadership That Works.*

35. Penny Bender Sebring and Anthony S. Bryk, "School Leadership and the Bottom Line in Chicago," *Phi Delta Kappan* 81, no. 6 (2000): 440–443.

36. Anthony S. Bryk et al., *Organizing Schools for Improvement: Lessons from Chicago* (Chicago: University of Chicago Press, 2010).

37. Rose M. Ylimaki, Stephen Jacobson, and Lawrie Drysdale, "Making a Difference in Challenging High-Poverty Schools: Successful Principals in the USA, England, and Australia," *School Effectiveness and School Improvement* 18, no. 4 (2007): 361–381.

38. Kathleen Brown et al., "Leading Schools of Excellence and Equity: Documenting Effective Strategies in Closing Achievement Gaps," *Teachers College Record* 113, no. 1 (2009): 57–96.

39. Ronald Ferguson et al., "How High Schools Become Exemplary: Ways That Leadership Raises Achievement and Narrows Gaps by Improving Instruction in 15 Public High Schools," *Report on the 2009 Annual Conference of the Achievement Gap Initiative at Harvard University,* http://www.agi.harvard.edu.

40. George Theoharis, "Disrupting Injustice: Principals Narrate the Strategies They Use to Improve Their Schools and Advance Social Justice," *Teachers College Record* 112, no. 1 (2010), 331–373.

41. Kenneth Leithwood et al., "How Leadership Influences Student Learning," http://www.wallacefoundation.org.

42. Karen Seashore Louis et al., "Learning from Leadership: Investigating the Links to Improved Student Learning," http://www.wallacefoundation.org.

3. At the Starting Gate

1. Rose McNeese, Thelma Roberson, and Geoffrey Haines, "Motivation and Leadership: A Comparison of Motivation Factors for Pursuing a Degree in Education Administration," *Connexions,* April 28, 2009, http://cnx.org/content/m22627/1.1.

2. Jared Coopersmith, "Characteristics of Public, Private, and Bureau of Indian Education Elementary and Secondary School Teachers in the United States: Results

from the 2007–08 Schools and Staffing Survey (NCES 2009-324)," National Center for Education Statistics, Institute of Education Sciences, U.S. Department of Education, Washington, DC. Available for download at http://nces.ed.gov/pubsearch/pubsinfo.asp?pubid=2009324.

3. Laura Hamilton, Mark Berends, and Brian Stecher, "Teachers' Responses to Standards-Based Accountability" (WR-259-EDU), Rand Corporation, April 2005.

4. Christina Theokas, "Shut Out of the Military: Today's High School Education Does Not Mean You Are Ready for Today's Army" (Washington, DC: The Education Trust, 2010).

4. First Things First

1. James S. Coleman, "Equality of Educational Opportunity (EEOS)," 1966. Although Coleman did not find that schools have no effect, his work did find that family background plays a large role in academic achievement. That finding set off a long line of research that has downplayed the role that schools can play.

2. Ronald R. Edmonds, "Effective Schools for the Urban Poor," *Educational Leadership,* October 1979.

3. Douglas B. Reeves, "High Performance in High Poverty Schools: 90/90/90 and Beyond," http://www.sjboces.org/nisl.

4. Richard Elmore, "Building a New Structure for School Leadership," Albert Shanker Institute, 2000.

5. Gardiner Morse, "Health Care Needs a New Kind of Hero: An Interview with Atul Gawande," *Harvard Business Review*, April 2010.

6. For a detailed description of the supervision process at Elmont, see *Supportive Supervision: Becoming a Teacher of Teachers*, Albert J. Coppola, Diane B. Scricca, and Gerard E. Conners (Corwin Press with the National Association of Secondary School Principals, 2004).

7. Read 180 is an intervention program designed to get students caught up in reading. For more information, go to http://read180.scholastic.com/reading-intervention-program.

8. Daniel Weisberg et al., "The Widget Effect," The New Teacher Project, 2009.

5. The Job That Never Goes Away

1. Susanna Loeb, Eileen Horng, and Daniel Klasik, "Principal's Time Use and School Effectiveness," *American Journal of Education* 116, no. 4 (2010): 491–523.

2. Robert Pianta et al., "Opportunities to Learn in America's Elementary Classrooms," *Science*, 30 March 2007, 1795–1796.

3. *What Works Clearinghouse Intervention Report: Reading Recovery*, United States Department of Education, Institute of Education Sciences, March 19, 2007.

4. Jeannie Oakes, *Keeping Track: How Schools Structure Inequality* (New Haven: Yale University Press, 1985).

5. Matthew Steinberg, Elaine Allensworth, and David W. Johnson, *Student and Teacher Safety in Chicago Public Schools: The Roles of Community Context and School Social Organization* (Chicago: Chicago Consortium on School Research, 2011).

6. Richard DuFour, Rebecca DuFour, Robert Eaker, and Gayle Karhanek, *Whatever It Takes: How Professional Learning Communities Respond When Kids Don't Learn* (Bloomington, IN: Solution Tree, 2004).

6. The Really Tough Stuff

1. Charles M. Payne, *So Much Reform, So Little Change: The Persistence of Failure in Urban Schools* (Cambridge, MA: Harvard Education Press, 2008).

2. Lt. Gen. Walter F. Ulmer Jr., "Leaders, Managers, and Command Climate," *Armed Forces Journal International*, July 1986. Courtesy of Tom Ricks's military blog, The Best Defense, http://ricks.foreignpolicy.com.

3. N. Suad Nasir, A. Jones, and M. McLaughlin, "School Connectedness for Students in Low-income Urban High Schools." *Teachers College Record* 113, no. 8 (2011): 120.

4. Payne, *So Much Reform.*

5. E. E. Werner, *Vulnerable but Invincible: A Longitudinal Study of Resilient Children and Youth* (New York: McGraw-Hill, 1982).

7. The Other Really Tough Stuff

1. National Policy Board for Educational Administration, *Educational Leadership Policy Standards: ISLLC 2008* (Washington, DC: Council of Chief State School Officers, 2008).

Conclusion

1. Kenneth Leithwood et al., "How Leadership Influences Student Learning," http://www.wallacefoundation.org.

2. Charles M. Payne, *So Much Reform, So Little Change: The Persistence of Failure in Urban Schools* (Cambridge, MA: Harvard Education Press, 2008).

3. We stole this metaphor from the medical field, which has been wrestling with an analogous problem of moving from a profession entirely dependent on individual practitioners to one where different specialties all work together to improve patient health. Dr. Atul Gawande has been one of the most prolific advocates that doctors need to be part of pit crews rather than act like cowboys and has written and spoken about it often, including it in his commencement address to the Harvard Medical School: "Cowboys and Pit Crews," *New Yorker* (May 26, 2011).

About the Authors

Karin Chenoweth is writer-in-residence at The Education Trust. She is the author of *It's Being Done: Academic Success in Unexpected Schools* (2007), which was named by Education Next as one of the top education books of the decade, and *How It's Being Done: Urgent Lessons from Unexpected Schools* (2009), both published by Harvard Education Press. A longtime education writer, she has written for a wide variety of publications including the *Washington Post, Education Week, American Educator,* and *Black Issues in Higher Education* (now *Diverse*).

Christina Theokas is director of research at The Education Trust. She holds a PhD in child development from Tufts University, where her research focused on understanding what characteristics of families, schools, and communities promote positive development in youth. Prior to joining The Education Trust, she worked in the research and evaluation office in Alexandria City Public Schools in Alexandria, Virginia. She evaluated programs and trained principals and teachers how to understand and use available data to make instructional decisions and to guide school reform efforts. In addition, she spent ten years working in schools in various capacities including as a special education teacher, school psychologist, and supervisor of the middle school program at a special education school in Massachusetts. She focused on developing curricula and programs to meet the social, emotional, and learning needs of diverse students.

Index